# WORLD AFFAIRS AND
# THE COLLEGE CURRICULUM

# Studies in
# Universities and World Affairs—

AMERICAN COLLEGE LIFE AS EDUCATION IN WORLD
OUTLOOK
*Howard E. Wilson*

FOREIGN STUDENTS AND HIGHER EDUCATION IN THE
UNITED STATES
*Cora Du Bois*

THE UNIVERSITY, THE CITIZEN, AND WORLD AFFAIRS
*Cyril O. Houle and Charles A. Nelson*

TRAINING OF SPECIALISTS IN INTERNATIONAL
RELATIONS
*C. Dale Fuller*

INTERNATIONAL RELATIONS IN INSTITUTIONS OF
HIGHER EDUCATION IN THE SOUTH
*Fred Cole*

UNIVERSITY RESEARCH ON INTERNATIONAL AFFAIRS
*John Gange*

WORLD AFFAIRS AND THE COLLEGE CURRICULUM
*Richard N. Swift*

AMERICAN UNIVERSITIES IN WORLD AFFAIRS:
A GENERAL REPORT
*Howard E. Wilson and Francis J. Brown*

# World Affairs
# and the
# College
# Curriculum

RICHARD N. SWIFT
*Associate Professor of Government*
*New York University*

AMERICAN COUNCIL ON EDUCATION • *Washington, D. C.*

*Prepared for the Carnegie Endowment for International Peace;
published by the American Council on Education*

LIBRARY OF CONGRESS CATALOG CARD NO. 59-13499
PRINTED IN THE UNITED STATES OF AMERICA

# Foreword

FOR OVER A DECADE, the place of world affairs in the undergraduate curriculum has been a matter of growing concern to the colleges and to organizations and individuals actively interested in American education. World War II and the succeeding years revealed a need both for specialists trained in international affairs and for increased awareness on the part of the general public of the complexities of world problems. Many colleges responded to these dual needs quickly, but too often without adequate forethought. Curricular and administrative difficulties were created—in part because of the pace at which new courses were introduced and in part because of changes of emphases within the field itself.

This study on curriculum is a direct outgrowth of a program initiated by the Carnegie Endowment for International Peace in 1950. At that time exploratory surveys were made by eight cooperating institutions for the purpose of evaluating the impact of world affairs on their respective campuses. On completion of the surveys, regional conferences were held to encourage further institutional self-appraisal. More than seventy institutions responded to this survey invitation. The final development of the program consists of topical studies that relate and summarize the different aspects touched upon and indicated by the completed surveys. This particular volume is the seventh such study.

*World Affairs and the College Curriculum* takes a broad look at the place of world affairs in the undergraduate curricula of

v

American colleges. While dealing with the requirements of the student majoring in this field, the volume is equally concerned with the utilization of the entire curriculum—physical sciences, social sciences, humanities—to prepare each student for a responsible understanding of the world in which he lives. World affairs, broadly conceived, can form a part of every course the student takes.

To treat this subject successfully, it was necessary to find an author who combined substantive knowledge of the field of world affairs with academic experience, particularly in curriculum development. Richard N. Swift fills both requirements. Dr. Swift is associate professor of government at New York University and was, from 1957–59, chairman of the Committee on Educational Policy of the Washington Square College of New York University. He also served as chairman of the Directing Committee, which devised the Program of Coordinated Liberal Studies, adopted by the college faculty in 1956. It is my hope that Dr. Swift's analysis of the current place of world affairs in the undergraduate curriculum and his suggestions for further development in this field will be of value to colleges in their examination of their curricula.

JOSEPH E. JOHNSON, *President*
*Carnegie Endowment for International Peace*

# *Preface*

MAN'S QUEST FOR KNOWLEDGE has already made it possible for him to propel satellites into outer space, and he is apparently on the verge of learning how he himself can travel safely to the moon and beyond. In fact, it seems likely that he will learn how to escape from the earth long before he finds out how to solve its problems. In the meantime, terrestrial difficulties become more and more serious as man releases the power of the atom and raises the specter of future wars of inestimable horror.

In a world so superbly equipped for mass suicide, awesome responsibilities fall upon the institutions man has established to develop culture and preserve ultimate values. They must alert us to the dangers we face, keep us aware of our obligations to diminish the threats confronting civilization, and guide us toward the knowledge and wisdom which can help us surmount present and future crises. Colleges and universities particularly, as custodians of man's heritage, must consider how to shape their curricula to perform these tasks. They must determine how best to embrace, within a tradition going back to the Middle Ages and before, the widely varied products of our troubled world: modern art and music, nuclear physics, and the global complexities of contemporary society.

Exactly how best to study all these subjects is highly controversial, and no subject causes more polemics than world affairs. The debate is especially lively in the United States, which has only recently found itself in the forefront of international politics. And coping with the issues is difficult because, in a nation with a highly decentralized educational system, liberal arts and professional faculties have naturally found diverse ways of teaching students about world affairs.

In *World Affairs and the College Curriculum,* I have tried to describe the problems colleges have had in attempting to define world affairs. Naturally, I have not been able to mention every worthwhile program in world affairs, but I have tried to illustrate with examples the several approaches colleges and universities have employed in teaching the subject. I have described the subject itself and pointed to a number of issues relating to it: to what extent college faculties should concern themselves with world affairs, how colleges can demonstrate their concern in their course offerings, whether world affairs is an appropriate subject for a major, and how colleges can present such a concentration. My study has led me to conclude that before American colleges can teach effectively about world affairs throughout the land, we must resolve a number of difficulties inherent in the nation's educational system.

In treating all these matters, I have benefited from many sources of information and enlightenment: the mimeographed and printed studies in the "Universities and World Affairs" series; many materials gathered together by the Carnegie Endowment for International Peace; correspondence with colleagues in other institutions; talks with foundation officials; and many writings on world affairs published before and since World War II. All of these sources have been extremely valuable, although no one either reads about or analyzes college curricula without certain caveats. Under optimal conditions, reliable information about curricula is extremely difficult to obtain. The ideal is always far easier to write about than to achieve, so that there are often discrepancies between reality and the image of curricula in college catalogues and course syllabi. And because the search for the ideal requires one to make changes as he goes along, instructors describing what they did one year cannot guarantee that they will do the same thing again the next. If, therefore, some of the courses or programs described here have already been superseded, the reader will, I trust, be indulgent. Hopefully, colleges will have profited from experiments now in progress, and new courses will represent another step on the road to finding satisfactory answers to very difficult problems. If this volume helps to further an exchange of ideas on how best to include the study of world affairs in the college curriculum and if it encourages others to address themselves to the issue, perhaps that is enough.

In addition to the persons whose work and writings I have gratefully acknowledged in footnotes, I should like to thank—without burdening them with my own shortcomings—those who have called to my attention materials and experiments in progress and have been especially helpful: Vincent Baker, who, before he rejoined the Department of State, gathered together many of the raw materials placed at my disposal when I began this study; Joseph E. Johnson, William G. Avirett, Lawrence S. Finkelstein, and Anne Winslow, of the Carnegie Endowment for International Peace, who have given me their confidence and have assisted me in many ways; William Marvel of the Carnegie Corporation, Kenneth W. Thompson of the Rockefeller Foundation, and Clarence Thurber of the Ford Foundation, who have talked with me from time to time about matters of mutual interest; and Howard E. Wilson, who, as general editor of this series, has given me considerable sound advice. Finally, I should like to thank Morton N. Cohen, of the City College of New York, whose continuing encouragement and editorial counsel have been indispensable.

RICHARD N. SWIFT

February 17, 1959

# Contents

# CHAPTER ONE

# What Are World Affairs?

The world, which took but six days to make, is like to take
six thousand to make out.

SIR THOMAS BROWNE, *Christian Morals*

N<small>O ONE UNDERTAKES</small> to study or teach about world affairs without asking what the words mean. The expression seems to embrace everything on earth, and if it does, it clearly refers, not to some one body of knowledge incorporated in a course, but rather to entire curricula. The facts of world affairs are unlimited not only in space but also in time, for since the world has existed for millions of years and may, with luck, persist for millions more, world affairs are the past and future as well as the present.

We may well inquire, as Alice did of Humpty Dumpty, whether you can make words mean so many different things and wish that we might reply with the arrogance of the Looking-Glass "egghead" that the question really is "which is to be master—that's all." Unfortunately, the world beyond the looking glass is not ours, and no epigram will solve our problem. We must attempt, rather, to determine just what world affairs are, and then we can ask about their place in the college curriculum.

In the broadest sense, world affairs do begin with the creation of the earth or even before, but we can, if only for convenience, agree that a large part of world affairs in this broad sense is not primarily the concern of social scientists, but of astronomers, geologists, archaeologists, and historians. It is history, in fact, that tells us that, although men have cooperated and fought with each other ever since history began, international relations, often used synonymously with world affairs, are, by any reckoning, very recent. The first significant milestone in relations among states, the Peace of Westphalia, stands at 1648. The landmark was not easily reached; so complicated were the numerous religious and political conflicts of the bitter Thirty Years War, it took the representatives of France, Sweden, Spain, and the Holy Roman Empire a full five years even to negotiate the treaty. By its terms the emperor surrendered his primary rights over much of his territory to the princes of the Empire. He also gave the princes the right to conclude alliances with one another and with foreign powers, so long as the pacts were not directed against him, and he granted independence to the republics of the United Netherlands and Switzerland. In making these inroads on the imperial authority, the negotiators, whether they realized it or not, had in fact assisted at the birth of the modern nation-state, and therefore, literally, of international relations.

The medieval dream of "one church–one state" was so strong, however, that the Empire survived, at least in name, into the nineteenth century, and it was almost one hundred and fifty years after Westphalia before Jeremy Bentham coined the word "international" to distinguish the law among sovereign nations from the Roman idea of a *ius gentium* among the peoples united under the symbol of the fasces.[1]

Given the recent origins of the international concept, it is not surprising that there was no general interest before the twentieth century, either in the United States or Europe, in studying international affairs formally. True, some scholars had concerned themselves with international law or the *ius gentium* from time

---

[1] "Penal Branch of Jurisprudence," *An Introduction to the Principles of Morals and Legislation* (1789), chap. xvii, sec. 25. Bentham gives the credit for the original observation that *droit des gens* ought to be *droit entre les gens* to the Chancellor of France D'Aguesseau in *Oeuvres*, II (1773), 337.

to time since the days of Rome,[2] and other scholars taught about the nonlegal relations among states in university courses in diplomatic history. But as world affairs became more complex, some academic outriders felt fenced in by law and history, and one of them, Paul S. Reinsch, blazed a new trail when in 1900 he offered his lectures in Contemporary Politics at the University of Wisconsin.[3] Clark University offered an undergraduate course in Contemporary History in 1908,[4] and the State University of Iowa and the University of Illinois widened the new path by offering courses in World Politics as early as 1913.

World War I naturally had a tremendous impact upon academic life in the United States, and perhaps more than anything else spurred scholars to investigate systematically the relations among states which had erupted into so tragic a holocaust. Before the war academic concerns with politics were primarily local. At the turn of the century, for instance, the curriculum in the schools of one American city included a six-month study of city ward politics and a two-month study of state politics. "Whatever time was left over at the end of the year," James T. Shotwell recalls, "was devoted to a hurried description of the complicated machinery of the national government,"[5] and there was no time at all for world affairs. But after the United States entered the war in 1917, American social scientists began to real-

[2] See Arthur Nussbaum, *A Concise History of the Law of Nations* (New York: Macmillan Co., 1947) for a convenient account of this subject.

[3] The lectures simultaneously appeared in *World Politics at the End of the Nineteenth Century Influenced by the Oriental Situation* (New York: Macmillan Co., 1900). Professor Reinsch also broke new ground in his *Public International Unions* (Boston: World Peace Foundation, 1911), a precursor of texts in international organization. See Merle Curti and Vernon R. Carstensen, *The University of Wisconsin: A History, 1848–1925* (Madison: University of Wisconsin Press, 1949), I, 630–40.

[4] S. H. Bailey, *International Studies in Modern Education* (London: Oxford University Press, 1938), p. 3.

[5] Shotwell, "Introduction," in Farrell Symons, *Courses on International Affairs in American Colleges, 1930–31* (Boston: World Peace Foundation, 1931), pp. x, xi.

ize that they must take a world view of politics and history. The change in perspective was radical, likened by Professor Shotwell to the one that took place in the Renaissance when theologians and philosophers awoke to the glories of ancient Greece and Rome. This time, however, the horizon widened to include not the nations of a rediscovered past, but those of the contemporary world.[6]

During World War I, American universities, especially in the Midwest and Far West began to offer courses entitled variously International Relations or International Politics. And with Parker T. Moon's lectures on Imperialism and World Politics at Columbia University in 1917, international relations established another stronghold in the East. Abroad, scholarly interest in world affairs affected course offerings, and the first European chair in international politics was established at the University of Wales in 1919.[7]

Closely allied to the scholars' interest in the world around them were their hopes for the future, inspired largely by Wilsonian idealism and the founding of the League of Nations, which, to many observers, seemed to offer people a new and startling way of conducting their political relations. Much of the teaching and research in international relations in the interwar years consequently now seems to have been excessively sentimental, Utopian, and idealistic. Many instructors stressed so much the new kind of world order, of which the League was supposed to be a harbinger, that they were severely shaken and their teaching was badly discredited when the events leading up to World War II showed that international cooperation, important though it might be, was by no means the dominant international motif. Having been excessively moralistic, students of international relations became excessively cynical in the late thirties, and only

[6] *Ibid.*, pp. viii, xi, xii.

[7] Grayson Kirk, *The Study of International Relations in American Colleges and Universities* (New York: Council on Foreign Relations, 1947), pp. 2–5; Hans J. Morgenthau and Kenneth W. Thompson, *Principles and Problems of International Politics* (New York: Alfred A. Knopf, 1950), [p. 3].

since World War II have they almost universally attempted to achieve a kind of objectivity appropriate to what they hope will continue to be a scientific study of society.[8]

Partly because international relations has emerged as a separate area of study so recently, but also by its very nature, its substance and limits are not very well defined. The academic communities which must decide whether to instruct their students in international relations therefore face difficult theoretical and practical problems: what the subject is, who should teach it, and how it should be taught. Without a definition, academic and administrative confusion is rife.

Most academicians consider international relations a branch of political science, agreeing with Grayson Kirk that the "focus of attention must be on intergovernmental relations and all things which affect them" because other types of relations, "i.e., private business and cultural relations, take on meaning for the student in the field chiefly as they affect international politics."[9] And distinguished members of the political science fraternity endorse Kirk's view that

the study of international politics centers around an analysis of national power, an understanding of the means by which international relations are conducted and conflicts of interest adjusted, and an evaluation of the philosophical, legal and moral bases, not merely of the present state of world development, but those of an emerging world society.[10]

8 For the sources of idealism in teaching about international relations immediately after World War I, see E. H. Carr, *The Twenty Years' Crisis, 1919–1939* (New York: Macmillan Co., 1939), Part II; see also Kirk, p. 4. For examples of the reaction to moralism and legalism see Hans Morgenthau, *In Defense of the National Interest* (New York: Alfred A. Knopf, 1951); and George F. Kennan, *American Diplomacy, 1900–1950* (Chicago: University of Chicago Press, 1951). For comments on the effect of these movements on the field of international relations, see Kirk, p. 4; Georg Schwarzenberger, *Power Politics* (New York: Frederick Praeger, 1951), pp. 8–9; Ernest Lefever, *Ethics and United States Foreign Policy* (New York: Meridian Books, 1957), chap. i; and Dwight Waldo, *Political Science in the United States of America* (Paris: Unesco, 1956), chap. v.

9 Kirk, p. 9.

10 Kirk, p. 14; for the views of the Committee for the Advancement of

The claims of political science for embracing international relations as one of its four branches[11] are very real on grounds both of history and logic. Political scientists were first to recognize how important it was to make independent studies of the relations among states, and they have nurtured the study of international relations within their departments. They have studied closely the politics of the interwar period, the way two great superpowers emerged after 1945 to dominate world affairs, and the rising forces of nationalism in Asia and Africa. The study of relations among states does properly concern them, and it is quite literally true, as Robson says, that "without the national state there could be no study of international relations."[12]

As many political scientists see it, they and the international relations specialists share the same subject matter, methods, and purposes, and any distinction between them is "purely one of emphasis and specialization."[13] International relations must rest upon "a solid foundation of political science."[14] Political scientists know that international relations are wider than the nation-state and politics, and "no one supposes," to quote Robson again, "that everything which is or can be included in international relations could be taught by political scientists." They insist, nonetheless, that it is "a political science subject"[15] and would undoubtedly approve the statements in two of the companion volumes in this series that international relations are "those activities in the intercourse of nation-states which make for war or

---

Teaching, see American Political Science Association, *Goals for Political Science, 1951* (New York: Dryden Press, 1951), p. 49. See also B. H. M. Vlekke, *On the Study of International Political Science* (London: David Davies Memorial Institute of International Studies [1957]), especially p. 14.

[11] The other three, according to the International Political Science Association, are political theory; government; and parties, groups, and public opinion. See William A. Robson, *The University Teaching of Social Sciences: Political Science* ([Paris]: Unesco, 1954), p. 66.

[12] *Ibid.*, p. 53.
[13] *Ibid.*, p. 63.
[14] *Loc. cit.*
[15] *Ibid.*, p. 65.

peace"[16] or "those studies which can lead to an understanding of contacts, connections, and intercourse between sovereign states in the modern world."[17]

As formidable contenders as political scientists are for the title of guardians of the study of international relations, their franchise is not so irrevocable as they sometimes make it appear. After all, they themselves have successfully maintained their claim to teach about politics only since about 1900. Before the turn of the century, economists and historians exercised that prerogative and, with arguments like those which political scientists use today against international relations specialists, resisted the attempts of political scientists to strip political analysis away from the older academic disciplines.[18]

Political scientists have, however, made distinguished contributions to man's understanding of politics, and most scholars today admit that a specialized approach to studying politics is valid. To concede the value of the political scientists' work is, however, by no means to give them prescriptive rights to the subjects they study. A college or university cannot grant them a continuing warrant to pre-empt the field of international relations unless in fact it can make no better arrangements. Society will always find political analysis essential, but scholars must not blind themselves to the usefulness of other approaches in analyzing even the nation-state.

A research team at Princeton University studying decision-making in international politics has illustrated well the need to take a flexible approach to world affairs. To carry on its research, the team "found it necessary to manufacture [its] . . . own scheme

[16] C. Dale Fuller, *Training of Specialists in International Relations* (Washington: American Council on Education, 1957), p. ix.

[17] Fred Cole, *International Relations in Institutions of Higher Education in the South* (Washington: American Council on Education, 1958), p. 1.

[18] Anna Haddow, *Political Science in American Colleges and Universities, 1636–1900* (New York: Appleton-Century Co., 1939) gives an account of the emerging discipline of political science.

of analysis by drawing on works and methods of scholars not normally consulted by political scientists," using "tools appropriate to the enterprise *regardless of their origin*."[19] Its report goes on to describe enough drawbacks in the several current approaches to international politics to convince any skeptic that although political science can help us understand international affairs, significant research (and, by inference, teaching) may well require scholars to move outside it.[20]

The Princeton team's interdisciplinary approach is particularly impressive because they frankly focused on a political process, on the behavior of the "decision makers," whose action is in effect the action of the state.[21] But though they were analyzing international political relations (all relationships "of political significance whether strictly political or not"[22]), they still found it necessary to draw on fields outside of politics—sociology, psychology, and philosophy. Their study and the work of other behavioral scientists provide admirable examples of the wisdom of taking the broadest possible view of international relations and make it clear that the ordinary political scientist's education would not train him for and might even blind him to the possibilities of using research data outside his own field.[23]

One could go even further than the Princeton team and point out that it is theoretically possible that its own research might have been more fruitful if it did not emphasize the state so much. As the political scientists themselves teach, nation-states as we know them today did not always exist, and there is no reason to assume that they are eternal. Concentrating on them in studying

---

[19] Richard C. Snyder, H. W. Bruck, and Burton Sapin, *Decision-Making as an Approach to the Study of International Politics* ("Foreign Policy Analysis Series," No. 3 [Princeton, N.J.: Organizational Behavior Section, Princeton University, 1954]), [p. i.]; italics mine.

[20] *Ibid.,* pp. 14–29.

[21] *Ibid.,* p. 118.

[22] *Loc. cit.*

[23] See Waldo, pp. 58–60 for a discussion of behavioralism in international relations.

world affairs, as political scientists naturally do, may lead scholars up blind alleys, or at least obscure other important phenomena. There are already some who seem to speak from vantage points offering wider perspectives than political science alone. Quincy Wright, for instance, points out that among peoples there have always been relations that are not official, legal, and diplomatic— for instance, the relations of traders, financiers, and missionaries; of students, teachers, and tourists. Other contacts have come about as people have migrated, and, more recently, as the representatives of the press, radio, films, and television have gone about their work. Nongovernmental organizations in the nineteenth and twentieth centuries also have had an active life of their own. Kirk embraces all these elements within political science,[24] but Wright suggests that there is a universal community to which numerous groups and even individuals belong. He would therefore not restrict studies of international relations to contacts among sovereigns or among political and territorial units. Rather, he believes it more scientific to include in international relations "the relations of all groups exercising some degree of independent power or initiative."[25] He concedes that the central interest in international relations today is in the relations between sovereign states, but believes it legitimate to investigate also such relations as those between pope and emperor in the Middle Ages and among the cities of antiquity.

Howard E. Wilson's use of the terms " 'world affairs' and 'international relations' . . . in the broadest sense" comes close to this view by including, "not only the politics of intergovernmental relations and the economics of international life, but also the cultural contacts and interpenetrations of peoples in contact with peoples." Thus, he says that "education for world affairs includes the understanding and attitudes students acquire respect-

---

[24] See *supra*, p. 5.
[25] Wright, *The Study of International Relations* (New York: Appleton-Century-Crofts, 1955), p. 8.

ing other cultures or world areas, and it includes understanding and feeling about America's position in the international situation." [26]

All these definitions of international relations or world affairs are, however, unsatisfactory because one cannot be sure just which relations to study in considering world problems and because the commonly used terms are either too narrow (international relations) or too broad (world affairs). [27] The wider definition is, however, more useful to those who believe that new and significant relations among men are emerging out of the work of international organizations such as the United Nations and its specialized agencies, the North Atlantic Treaty Organization, the European Coal and Steel Community, and the newer Common Market and Euratom. [28] Whether in the future world affairs as a field of study will deal primarily with regions, universal political parties, or interest groups, [29] one cannot positively predict, but it would seem wise even for political scientists to remain alert for such a possibility and not commit themselves irrevocably to the nation-state. Even if we agree that "crucial conflicts and adjustments generated by interaction express themselves primarily *politically*," [30] and that the nation-state is the leading international political phenomenon of our time, we tend unwisely, by stressing

26 Wilson, *American College Life as Education in World Outlook* (Washington: American Council on Education, 1956), p. xii.

27 See Wright, *The Study of International Relations*, pp. 6–7, for an excellent discussion of the semantic difficulties involved.

28 See, for instance, Philip Jessup, *Transnational Law* (New Haven, Conn.: Yale University Press, 1956), and "Report of the Committee on Review of the Charter of the United Nations," in *Proceedings and Committee Reports of the American Branch of the International Law Association, 1955–1956* (New York: New York University Law Center, 1956), pp. 69–81; Quincy Wright, *Contemporary International Law* (New York: Doubleday & Co., 1955), especially chaps. 4 and 5; and Karl W. Deutsch *et al., Political Community and the North Atlantic Area* (Princeton, N.J.: Princeton University Press, 1957).

29 Wright, *The Study of International Relations*, p. 6.

30 Cole, p. 13. See also Hans J. Morgenthau, "Area Studies and the Study of International Relations," *International Social Science Bulletin*, IV (1952), 11, for a very forceful statement of the position that "among the many foci

nation-states and the political process, to discount or ignore cultural or psychological conflicts. Nor should we depreciate such matters as the success and failure of international law and organization or the impact on world affairs of geography, economics, or psychology.[31] As important as it is for scholars to investigate state behavior, they must also take other approaches to world affairs in the interest of teaching and research.

Those who conceive of international relations less in terms of politics and the nation-state and more in terms of world tensions, their causes, and the possible means of abating them[32] consider political science to have been a useful springboard for teaching and research, but one which has now become too rigid. They desire therefore to have the academic world recognize international relations as a separate field of study with an independent status. They want the student of international relations to concentrate on what Chevallier calls *"le complexe relationnel international."* By *le complexe* Chevallier means the "tangled intertwining of relationships arising in all sorts of fields, among the various States" in international society and also, secondarily, the relationships between the states and international organizations. To describe and analyze the *complexe,* one needs to know diplomatic history and international law, and also political, ideologi-

---

of international relations [the] most important from the theoretical and practical point of view [is] politics, conceived as a struggle for power among individuals and groups."

[31] See, for instance, Percy E. Corbett, *The Study of International Law* (New York: Doubleday & Co., 1955), p. 50: "The starting point [in studying international law] should be, not the assumption that the States of the world form a society, subject, like other societies to law, but simply the observable fact that individuals and groups are engaged in activities that do not terminate at geographical, political or racial boundaries." See also Charles de Visscher, *Theory and Reality in Public International Law,* trans. Percy E. Corbett (Princeton, N. J.: Princeton University Press, 1957).

[32] C. A. W. Manning, *The University Teaching of Social Sciences: International Relations* (Paris: Unesco, 1954), pp. 77–78. See also Geoffrey L. Goodwin, *The University Teaching of International Relations* (Oxford: Blackwell, 1951), pp. 27, 37.

cal, and economic history, along with geography, demography, sociology, economics, and other subjects as well.[33] Chevallier's formula contains no elements not in Kirk's or Robson's, but it gives first place to the *complexe* and puts less stress on politics and the role of the nation-state.

One fundamental problem which makes it difficult for its advocates to establish international relations as a discipline in its own right is that no one is quite sure just what a "discipline" is. Some believe that disciplines must have distinct subjects, methods, and purposes,[34] but such criteria would deny the title to most recognized academic disciplines. The closer one looks at any field of knowledge—economics, law, linguistics, mathematics, medicine, physics, zoology—the vaguer its boundaries seem, the more uncertain its scope, the greater the disagreements about its methods, and the more serious the doubts about the personnel who profess it and their qualifications.[35] In fact, even political scientists are suspect in England, and the term "political science," generally accepted in the United States, has been challenged as inaccurate in international gatherings by many foreign scholars.[36]

One may avoid the difficulty of qualifying international politics as a discipline by describing it instead as a "distinct subject" or as a "field of study."[37] George Kennan goes so far as to say that although international relations is a "subject" and not a discipline, "it is a mistake to think of [it] . . . as anything outside the

[33] J.-J. Chevallier, "L'enseignement des relations internationales," in *L'enseignement des Sciences Sociales en France* ([Paris]: Unesco, 1953), p. 115, translated in part and quoted in Manning, p. 10.

[34] Robson, pp. 62–63.

[35] For excellent discussions of this point, see Wright, *The Study of International Relations*, p. 24, and Cole, pp. 28–32.

[36] See Howard R. Bowen, "Graduate Education in Economics," *American Economic Review*, XLIII (1953), Supplement, Part 2, 102; A. H. Hanson, "Politics as a University Discipline," *Universities Quarterly*, VIII (1953), 34–35; William Ebenstein, "Toward International Collaboration in Political Science: A Report on the Unesco Project 'Methods in Political Science,'" *American Political Science Review*, XLII (1948), 1181–89.

[37] See Goodwin, p. 37, and Walter Sharp in Goodwin, p. 42.

regular context of life—as anything, that is, which a man could hope to understand without having to understand things more basic. . . . "[38] Kennan cautions the student of world affairs against thinking that one can comprehend world affairs by studying merely the intricacies of tariffs or treaties, charters or covenants, or by sampling opinion. One must understand the way governments act, but to him their behavior is that "of individual man in the political context, and of the workings of all those basic impulses—national feeling, charity, ambition, fear, jealousy, egotism, and group attachment—which are the stuff of his behavior in the community of other men." One must understand these basic patterns to know about world affairs. Such understanding comes, in Kennan's opinion, not from courses dealing exclusively with international affairs, but instead "from those things which have been recognized for thousands of years as the essentials of humanistic study: from history itself, and from all those more subtle and revealing expressions of man's nature that go by the name of art and literature." Kennan has gone on to follow his own advice in recent years by returning to historical studies, which he has found enormously rewarding.[39]

As Kennan indicates, the student of international relations must range far and wide. Delimiting the subject has become even more difficult since World War II because world affairs themselves have exerted great pressures upon academicians. The war, the establishment of the United Nations and its specialized agencies, and the attention governments have given to international public information activities have compelled scholars to look into new fields such as international education and communications

---

[38] Address at the 39th Annual Mid-Winter Meeting of the National Alumni Association of Princeton University, Feb. 21, 1953, as printed in the 83d Cong., 1st Sess., *Congressional Record*, Appendix, XCIX, Part 9, pp. A995–97. Kennan's views, as presented in the remainder of this paragraph, may be found in the text of this address.

[39] See, for example, his *Soviet-American Relations 1917–1920* (2 vols.; Princeton, N. J.: Princeton University Press, 1956 and 1958).

and the psychology and sociology of international relations. They have also had to revise their teaching of established fields such as international organization. The fission and fusion bombs and the new atomic technology have led many to reassess their ideas of war, power politics, and political geography. The cold war between the United States and the Soviet Union after World War II has accentuated the importance of these studies, as has the need of both government and business for trained personnel in the international field (although neither is sure just how best to train the personnel they want).[40] And students, attracted by the increasing number of educational and professional opportunities open to them after World War II, have made their own demands on college curricula.[41]

Like the universe itself, international relations seems to be constantly expanding, and once the specialists admit that the field embraces more than the purely political, they face the problem of where to draw the boundary lines or whether they can draw any lines at all. Librarians attempting to maintain international relations collections, for example, have tasks in some ways greater than those of Hercules. The twelve labors were, at least, well defined, but who can tell librarians how to keep their lists of works on international relations within bounds?[42] Putting limits on international relations this side of infinity may even be a logical impossibility if one takes literally the views of Sir Alfred Zimmern, first occupant of the Chair of International Politics at the University of Wales. Rather poetically, Sir Alfred warned all comers: "Let it never be forgotten that no academic regulations

[40] Haverford College, the Maxwell School (Syracuse University), and the Graduate School of Public Administration and Social Service (New York University) have undertaken programs specifically to train students for new fields in international administration.

[41] Wright, *The Study of International Relations,* pp. 27–28; see also *Goals,* p. 44.

[42] The Carnegie Endowment for International Peace disposed of its collections, both in Paris and Washington after World War II, in part at least because it could put no discernible, logical limitations on them.

can set frontiers to our study, which like the wind, bloweth where it listeth, and like the birds, can pick up seeds of wisdom in most unexpected quarters."[43] What Zimmern had in mind was that the study of international relations "extends from the natural sciences at one end to moral philosophy or even further at the other." Nothing is alien to it: physical geography, medical science, developments of physics, or moral philosophy; the banner of the study, in a paraphrase of Terence, is *"nihil humani aliena a nobis putamus."*[44]

To Zimmern, it appears that international relations does not have a single coherent body of teaching material, and one cannot compress it within a textbook. "It is not a single subject, but a bundle of subjects," a bundle of law, economics, political science, geography, and more besides. These subjects are not part of international relations, but some aspects of them are. The subjects are not, moreover, indiscriminately thrown together but viewed from a common angle. "Viewed from that angle," he continues, "one part of them is in the light, the rest remaining, as it were, in the shadow. The different subjects *converge*, so to speak, to a common point, a point from which the contemporary world of affairs can be observed."[45]

Zimmern's notion of the "common angle" is perhaps the strongest and most defensible position students of international relations have ever assumed. Time and time again they have reiterated the idea. One finds it in the works by Edith Ware, Grayson Kirk, Robert MacIver and Charles H. Page, C. A. W. Manning, Walter Sharp, Frederick S. Dunn, and Fred Cole.[46]

[43] Zimmern, "Introductory Report to the Discussions in 1935," in *University Teaching of International Relations* (Paris: International Institute of Intellectual Cooperation, 1939), p. 10. Portions of the essay have been reprinted in Morgenthau and Thompson, pp. 19–24.

[44] *Ibid.*, p. 8.

[45] *Ibid.*, p. 9.

[46] See Ware, *The Study of International Relations in the United States, Survey for 1934* (New York: Columbia University Press, 1934), p. 172; Kirk, pp. 11–12; MacIver and Page, *Society: An Introductory Analysis* (New York:

Unfortunately, while all social scientists pay tribute to the idea of a common angle or focus and to the interdependence of their subjects, there has been a counterbalancing trend in colleges and universities since the eighteenth century toward specialized teaching and research.[47] The trend away from the general view is especially ironical in the social sciences, in which the general view of the world has never been more important than it is now. In the study of international relations, however, one finds scholars attempting to reconstitute the general view of society.[48] It is in fact to recapture this whole view that Chevallier addressed himself to the *complexe relationnel international* and Manning stressed the centrality of international relations. They and their allies, however, have to fight against the established order of university departments with watertight barriers between them. Zimmern has said,

The question has been asked as to what the Founder of Christianity would do if he came back and saw the multiplicity of sects who invoke his name. Similarly one feels inclined to ask what Plato and Aristotle would do if they came back and found the multitudinous rags and tatters into which industrious specialists have divided the seamless garments of their thought. They would have to look in a dozen or more pigeonholes for some part of the study of their ideas; and they would find hardly any one who really understood them because hardly any one had studied them as a unity.[49]

Creating the most effective administrative arrangements for teaching about international relations is, however, not easy. The principal difficulties arise from the tendency of naturally conservative academicians sometimes to confuse the interests of good teaching and scholarship with their own parochial interests and to see specters where there are none. Some political scientists, for

---

Rinehart & Co., 1949), p. v, quoted in *Goals*, p. 131; Goodwin, p. 42; Manning, pp. 72–73; Cole, pp. 31–32, 58; and Dunn, "The Scope of International Relations," *World Politics*, I (1948), 143.

[47] See Bailey, p. 76.

[48] *Ibid.*, p. 77.

[49] Sir Alfred Zimmern, "Education and International Goodwill," *The Sixth Earl Grey Memorial Lecture* (London: Oxford University Press, 1924), pp. 15–16.

instance, warn that if international relations exists as a separate field, students of political science may learn nothing of international relations unless they specialize in it and students of international relations may learn nothing of political science. Such a dichotomy, they argue, "would be equally bad for students, for teachers, for research, and for the organum of the social sciences."[50] The dichotomy is, however, a false one, because the advocates of international relations emphasize that they do not wish to teach international relations apart from the various "underpinning disciplines."[51]

Political scientists also criticize the scholars whose principal interest is international relations for their inability to agree even on the limits of their study. Robson, for instance, notes that one group could not define the subject or its objective content, and complains about the "ambiguous and nebulous position occupied by international relations in the academic world."[52] On the other hand, what is one to make of the rather startling observation of Furniss that one "compelling reason" for allowing political science to be the center of any systematic study of international relations is "the amorphous nature of political science itself." In his opinion, it was exactly because political science embraced a wide variety of fields and because political scientists were unable to define precisely what their subject was, that political science departments were so admirably suited to be hosts for international relations.[53] Political science's virtue is apparently international relations' vice!

[50] Robson, p. 66.

[51] Goodwin, p. 37.

[52] Robson, pp. 62, 63. Robson based his observations on Manning's excellent account of the misgivings scholars have about international relations as a discipline, together with his own rebuttal of the principal arguments and the report of the consensus of a group of international relations specialists. See Goodwin, p. 27, and Manning, "International Relations, An Academic Discipline," in Goodwin, pp. 11–26.

[53] Edgar S. Furniss, Jr., "Theory and Practice in the Teaching of International Relations in the United States," in Goodwin, pp. 94–109.

Political scientists also allege that attempts to identify international relations as a field threaten the scope and integrity of political science. They are naturally concerned about political science—if they were not, who would be?—but they can hardly expect the rest of the world, even the academic world, to despair because an independent study of international relations might leave political science departments "weakened, . . . stripped of what is most essential in . . . personnel and structure," [54] by taking away from them such core subjects as sovereignty, power, nationalism, organization, and law. In actual fact, however, even the most ardent champions of the field of international relations do not want any college to jeopardize the integrity of political science.[55]

Arguments of academic jurisdiction are (or rather, should be) quite beside the point. The fate of political science or any other field of study is, after all, much less important than the fate of mankind. If, in order to come closer to truth, a college faculty finds it necessary in the future to reorganize or supplement departments in ways some political scientists oppose, it would be no more of a tragedy than it was for those historians and economists around the turn of the century when faculties reorganized in ways the political scientists favored. All academicians should recognize that to advance teaching and research, it may be necessary from time to time to create new departments within colleges and universities, rearrange courses, and make it possible for new combinations of scholars to work together more easily.

Effective teaching and scholarship are, after all, the principal goals of colleges and universities. How to define international relations and how to decide whether it is a separate discipline or part of political science are really secondary matters. But these controversies are relatively meaningless[56] only if educators regard

54 *Goals*, p. 66.
55 See Goodwin, *passim*.
56 See the discussion in Cyril O. Houle and Charles A. Nelson, *The Uni-*

departmental lines as matters of administrative convenience and not as customs barriers manned by intransigent *douaniers* who will let no traffic through or who allow the intellectual baggage to move in only one direction.

As Fred Cole has so well pointed out, curricular organization and departmental jurisdiction raise more problems than does the nature of international relations. Everyone concedes the inter-disciplinary character of international relations, and it is primarily because the student of international relations wants to find a way to devote adequate time to the several disciplines bearing on his subject and to apply the disciplines to the specific problems of international relations that he wishes to transcend existing de-partmental restrictions and requirements. Where the "ecumeni-cal view of the social sciences prevails," international relations flourishes regardless of administrative arrangements. However, "when such a view is not held, or is held in theory only, . . . there will be continued pressure on the part of international relations advocates to escape the bonds of departmental restrictions and to set up departments of their own."[57]

Everyone, it would seem, is ready to pour the soothing oils of integration upon the troubled departmental waters, but a perma-nent calm is unlikely. Adjusting disciplines within colleges and universities is bound to be a stormy matter, for, as Wright has pointed out, once textbooks and learned journals appear and universities establish academic chairs and curricula under given names and grant degrees, a discipline achieves a solidarity "diffi-cult to change however illogical or inconvenient [it] . . . may in time prove to be."[58]

Despite this evidence of human frailty, educational institutions must arrange for teaching and research in international affairs

---

*versity, the Citizen, and World Affairs* (Washington: American Council on Education, 1956), p. 19.

[57] Cole, p. 37.

[58] Wright, *The Study of International Relations*, p. 25.

to go forward in the most creative way possible, mobilizing their resources as may be necessary. If problems of world affairs are worth investigating at all, colleges must instruct students about them and organize the instruction so as to cast some light upon the problems for the benefit of the world at large. And one may hope that with the passage of years, academicians concerned with world affairs will be able to pay less attention to disciplinary divisions and more to the problems of substance and teaching that properly concern them.

One important issue is how most effectively to teach students about world affairs in liberal arts colleges. It is a problem for everyone concerned with the liberal arts: whether one believes that world affairs is a discipline of its own, a congeries of subjects, a subordinate part of political science or sociology, or an interdisciplinary subject, or takes no position on the question at all. It is moreover a problem in colleges which have departments of world affairs and committees on world affairs and for those which do not. It is quite appropriately the next problem to engage our attention.

# CHAPTER TWO

# World Affairs and the Liberal Arts

Common studies, pursued in the same spirit, in all civilized countries, form, beyond the restrictions of diverse and often hostile nationalities, a great country which no war profanes and no conqueror menaces.

GASTON PARIS, *Address,* College de France, 1870

COLLEGES HAVE for a long time been far more complex than the ideal log of wood with Mark Hopkins at one end and a student at the other, and as time goes on it becomes increasingly difficult to determine who should teach what and to whom. How a society answers these questions depends in large part on its nature and aspirations. Before we can decide whether anyone should study world affairs in college, therefore, we must first examine the nature of our society and the place of the college in it.

Perhaps the quality that most distinguishes twentieth-century societies from earlier ones is their interdependence. Almost everything that happens anywhere in the world today affects all men in all places. Technology, in creating the steam engine, telegraph, telephone, radio, and airplane, has for all practical purposes abolished distance and brought men, with all their prejudices and antagonisms, closer together than ever before. For modern vessels, the seas are much less like moats than highways, and for planes, they are mere ponds. "Overnight from New York to the major capitals of Europe" is the catch phrase of every transatlantic airline. Man's inventiveness has made it impossible for the United States to ignore world affairs or to shun the diplomatic game as if it were no more than the strategems of Machiavellis of the Old World. The nearness of Europe and Asia has put the frontiers of this country on the Rhine and the Yalu and has made what happens in China and Hungary, in the Soviet Union and France, in the Middle East and South Africa very important to the United States.

With distance annihilated, not only men and their goods move with ease around the world, but their ideas also travel fast and far, and they have given rise in international affairs to a new phenomenon—global ideological warfare. The values of democracy are on trial in the twentieth century before a larger jury than has ever before assembled to hear the case for freedom, and the cold war has dramatized the conflict in a way a twentieth-century democracy cannot ignore except at its peril. The citizens of the United States, consequently, must decide matters of grave importance, and their attitudes may make the difference between life and death for the individual, the nation, and even for civilization itself. These ordinary men and women must, in the long run, judge those who are responsible for decisions at Yalta and in the United Nations, for policies like the Truman and Eisenhower Doctrines, the Marshall Plan, Point Four, and Atoms for Peace, for discussions of disarmament, trade, recognition of Communist China, and for the use of the atom and hydrogen bombs. To the extent that citizens concern themselves with these critical problems, intelligent debate can safeguard democracy. If Americans suspend judgment on these questions, they surrender one of the major privileges of democratic citizenry, for democracy assumes that by sincere inquiry and rational debate, free men may hammer out a viable policy.[1] They may turn for advice

[1] See Walter Lippmann, "The Changing Times," in Leonard D. White (ed.), *The State of the Social Sciences* (Chicago: University of Chicago Press, 1956), p. 346, for an excellent discussion of this point.

to experts and trained specialists, but unless they would forfeit their freedom, they themselves must continue to evaluate the experts' work.

Citizen responsibility in a democracy is not simply a matter of abstract theory. It flows from the demonstrable truth that the shape of the world affects every man, so that all who would be free must help mold it. It is not enough in a democracy for engineers to design bridges, physicians to heal the sick, lawyers to prepare briefs, and businessmen to spin the wheels of commerce. They must all be more than competent merely in their specialties; they must also be intelligent citizens concerned with the major issues of their time in all fields.[2] All men together help determine whether the engineer spends his life in an air-conditioned office, planning highways to speed the peacetime traffic of the world, or in some wilderness building Bailey Bridges to move troops across rivers; whether the physician conducts research in well-equipped hospitals or performs operations at emergency first-aid stations behind the battle lines; whether lawyers help administer justice in courts of law or settle claims of civilians against military forces; whether scientists push forward on the major frontiers of theoretical research for creative purposes or concentrate on making more and more powerful weapons of destruction; whether businessmen develop consumer products for higher standards of living or manage military commissaries at base depots. The future of all young persons depends in part on their willingness to concern themselves with the question of survival in their own time. The challenge has been thrust upon them; world events will not let them ignore it; and their own eagerness to prepare for life involves them from the first days of maturity in a search for the answers to the world's dilemmas.

[2] Harold W. Dodds ("Liberal Arts, Challenge to Communism," in Association of American Colleges, *Bulletin*, XXXV [1949], 341), and Milton S. Eisenhower ("Education for International Understanding," *Educational Record*, XXXV [1954], 246) have written eloquently on the importance of world affairs for the average citizen.

Even if there were no possibility of war, this century would require everyone to be aware of the world at large. Progress in all fields depends on free access to ideas from all corners of the earth and on the ability of people in all walks of life to work successfully with their counterparts in other lands. To the extent that it has been impossible to exchange ideas internationally, men have wasted money, time, and effort, as for instance in the separate but parallel work done by the world's atomic physicists. Independently, they have often arrived at the same point without consulting one another (as they rediscovered in 1955 at the first International Conference on the Peaceful Uses of Atomic Energy), but how much more fruitful for science might their research be if they could freely work and confer together.

Whatever his interests, modern man must seek out the ideas of those outside his own community. What is more, his standard of living very much depends on many items which his nation cannot grow or manufacture at all or which other nations produce more efficiently. Even in so relatively self-sufficient a country as the United States, the citizen needs imports to live in the style to which he is accustomed.[3] No one can afford to hide from these facts of modern life; there is, to be sure, no place to hide.

Colleges, no less than individuals, must take account of our interdependence, and some are trying to do so realistically. Knowing that man will survive only if he understands the political and social forces in his world, many colleges and universities require their students to take certain courses specifically designed to prepare them for their role as citizens in a democracy, and some include new material on world affairs in courses traditionally required of all students. In spite of these developments, most students graduating from American colleges have not encountered world affairs as a cohesive unit within existing require-

[3] A very effective, popular presentation of this dependence can be found in U.S. Department of State, *Together We Are Strong*, Publication 6571 (Washington: Government Printing Office, 1957).

ments. Few take any courses specifically on world affairs, even when the college offers them as electives. As a result, many faculty members, when asked, say that they are graduating a significant number of students each year who are ignorant of world affairs. In one large state university a few years ago, for instance, only about fifteen liberal arts students in a graduating class of over one thousand had taken as many as three semester courses each relating to world affairs.

Actually most colleges have never really asked themselves specifically if their present offerings do equip students to participate in the great debates of their own time; and many believe that they are at present doing all they can to carry out their responsibilities when in fact they are not. The question has perhaps been posed too recently for colleges to consider it thoroughly. It is, after all, only since World War II that Americans have realized generally that their commitments to the world abroad were long-term ones which would continue into the indefinite future. World War I seemed to many people only a temporary interruption of the beneficent order of peaceful progress inherited from the nineteenth century, and to most Americans it made good sense as late as the 1930's to attempt through neutrality laws to shelter the nation from the war clouds gathering in Europe. Only since the bombs rained down on Pearl Harbor and World War II thrust the United States and the Soviet Union into the limelight has it become apparent to nearly all thinking Americans that they cannot extricate themselves from world affairs. No longer is it possible to think in terms of a Fortress America, a bastion cultivating in splendid isolation all the best elements of Western civilization. For better or for worse, we are joined in a common cause with the rest of the free world.

What America's role is and how to play it are questions of the utmost importance; they are among the great issues of our time; and, as such, they are questions of the first importance for the colleges and universities of the United States to consider if they are to do in the future, as they have done in the past: help man "break the intellectual chains that keep him a serf by binding him to his parish, by binding him to his narrow workaday tasks, by binding him to accept the authority of those placed over him in matters temporal and spiritual." American colleges and universities must try to make the American, like truly free men everywhere, "spiritually a citizen of all places and all times,"[4] must help him avoid "cultural and sectarian myopia . . . provincialism and prejudice," and must assist him to achieve the widest possible national and global perspectives.[5] Scholars must see that the debate on United States foreign policy is vigorous and informed, must contribute to it whenever possible, and must criticize the evidence and logic of the debaters outside the academic forum.[6]

Ever since the Middle Ages, colleges and universities have accepted the responsibility of helping to prepare students to face the major issues of their time. For the university of the twelfth century, for instance, the burning issues appertained to the nature of reality. Classes in the dialectic resounded with debate on whether the objects one saw and felt were real or only transitory examples of an all-embracing, abstract reality, a fundamental question for a people convinced that the universe was the scene of a great drama God had prepared for the human race. The university students of the twelfth century were primarily preparing for the clergy, although some would go into politics, law, and teaching. As future ecclesiastics, statesmen, lawyers, and teachers, they were set apart from the rest of the community, associating with it as little as possible, firmly convinced that learning was their special province, not to be entered upon by the common man

---

[4] Arthur Bestor, *The Restoration of Learning* (New York: Alfred A. Knopf, 1955), p. 38.

[5] Theodore M. Green, *Liberal Education Reconsidered* (Cambridge, Mass.: Harvard University Press, 1954), pp. 37–39.

[6] See Cyril O. Houle and Charles A. Nelson, *The University, the Citizen, and World Affairs* (Washington: American Council on Education, 1956), chap. 4; Lippmann, "The Changing Times," in White, p. 346; and Erwin Panofsky, "In Defense of the Ivory Tower," *Harvard Alumni Bulletin*, LIX (1957), 706–10.

without grave consequences. Books were in Latin, unintelligible to the masses, and a great gulf existed between the educated classes and the average man.

Two centuries later, man's principal preoccupations were transformed to suit an age of rapidly changing economic patterns, of new scientific awareness, of great achievements in art. The Renaissance scholars were devoted to "enlightenment," to cultivating and emancipating the individual from the slavish need to accept authority. They protested against the unwillingness of the medieval scholar to observe the world around him and conduct experiments. They could no longer accept the professor who read to his students from Aristotle that "The horse is a quadruped, swift of foot, with a long tail, two eyes and two nostrils and . . . teeth," and then turned seriously and sadly from his book to remark, "And so gentlemen we shall never know how many teeth the horse has." To the Renaissance university men, philosophizing on the nature of universals was much less important than discovering the best ways to fashion a man worthy of the new intellectual freedom of his time. The Renaissance university men looked about them, reveled in the rediscovered classical literature, and turned their eyes upon the wonders of nature and man. What they had in mind was captured well in 1392 by Vergerius, a teacher in arts at the University of Padua, who wrote of his contemporaries,

We call those studies *liberal* which are worthy of a free man; those studies by which we attain and practice virtue and wisdom; that education which calls forth, trains and develops those highest gifts of body and of mind which ennoble men, and which are rightly judged to rank next in dignity to virtue only.[7]

This Renaissance spirit has infused education in all later societies, including our own, where men aspire to be free. It came into the curriculum of the first college organized in the New World for those few students who could seek out a higher educa-

[7] William Harrison Woodward, *Vittorino da Feltre and Other Humanist Educators* (Cambridge: Cambridge University Press, 1897), p. 102.

tion in the colonies. The curriculum was prepared by Henry Dunster, president of four-year-old Harvard College, as a three-year course for the bachelor's degree, exercising the mind through logic, teaching a man to speak and write through rhetoric, and acquainting him with the great traditions and thoughts of the past through classical literature. Dunster prescribed "the Liberal Arts, the Three Philosophies [natural, moral, and metaphysical], and the Learned Tongues [Latin, Greek, and Hebrew]" as the curriculum to prepare young colonials to meet the needs of their times as an educated clergy.[8]

This Renaissance curriculum remained virtually unchanged for over a century, but new demands on education arose after the American Revolution. People in the young United States were poor and hard-working, and there were few leaders among them. Education was not widespread, and most citizens were too backward to realize how important it was. Both Washington and Jefferson did everything they could, however, to improve education and make it more accessible in order to guarantee that the future of the country would be in safe hands. Citizens of the new democracy would not find the classics and philosophy sufficient for their purposes, in Jefferson's view, and he urged his own college, William and Mary, to add science, history, law, political economy, and modern languages to meet the needs of nineteenth-century American democracy. Unsuccessful with his own alma mater, he founded the University of Virginia, which embraced his ideas when it opened in 1825 and stood in its early years as the fountainhead of progressive college education.[9]

The curriculum of American universities continued to adapt to the nation's changing needs. Colleges appeared throughout the land, responding to a national spirit, an intellectual awaken-

[8] Samuel Eliot Morison, *Three Centuries of Harvard* (Cambridge, Mass.: Harvard University Press, 1936), pp. 11, 29–31.

[9] Harold Underwood Faulkner, *American Political and Social History* (3rd ed.; New York: F. S. Crofts Co., 1943), pp. 215–16.

ing in the 1830's and 1840's, the expansive optimism of the West, and the continuing desire of the churches to train a ministry for a growing population. State universities sprang up to fulfill demands for education for the many, offering curricula primarily designed to cope with the agricultural and mechanical needs of a largely rural population. The liberal arts colleges followed the Jeffersonian precepts, preparing students for new careers in a rapidly changing society. College offerings burgeoned with English literature, history, economics, fine arts, music, philosophy, biology, chemistry, physics, and zoology. The seven liberal arts of medieval times proliferated into hundreds of courses as nineteenth-century European scholarship and research in science and the arts flooded into this country. To make available all the new learning to students, American colleges and universities adopted the elective system championed by President Charles W. Eliot of Harvard.

By setting before their students a richly varied educational fare, college and university faculties helped ensure to an industrializing nation the supply of specialists it needed. But educators knew that they were also graduating men either educated superficially in a variety of fields or so specialized that they no longer could claim the wisdom which was once the boast of educated men. How to combine the proper amounts of special and general education became the major question of twentieth-century education. First, colleges began to modify their unrestricted elective systems by requiring students to concentrate and distribute their courses in certain ways to acquire some depth in one or more related fields and to learn to appreciate knowledge outside their own specialties. Then, to counter a tendency to teach every subject in the curriculum as though designed solely to attract potential experts, a number of colleges introduced into their curricula, sometimes under the label of general education, courses in the humanities, the social sciences, and the natural sciences—broad, interdisciplinary courses attempting to bring together the essential materials of each field or the subject matter of several fields in a pattern most useful for the general student.

But the general education movement would appear not to be the end of the search for the best pattern of courses for students in modern America. Critics of the movement have been quick to object that some general education courses were denuded of intellectual garb, substantial content, and a body of fact. Opponents of present educational trends charge that "many programs of general education are devised in whole or in part for students whose intellectual capacity may be too meager to justify either admission to advanced levels of liberal study or to a professional curriculum,"[10] that they consist of "rambling, catch-all courses, geared to the meager abilities of the marginal student. . . . complete educational inanity,"[11] and that they are "an avant-garde excuse for intellectual laxity and somnolence."[12] On the other hand, the Harvard Committee report on general education, which gave so much impetus to the general education movement, did not at any point recommend lowering educational standards, and, as one observer has noted, "if liberal education is broadly conceived in terms of its relevance to human living in our time, the difference between liberal and general education is mainly one of degree."[13]

While the general education problem persists, new experiments are already in progress to free students from much of the paraphernalia of courses and grades and to help them fashion individual or group reading programs in what seems to be an at-

[10] T. R. McConnell, "General Education: An Analysis," in Nelson B. Henry (ed.), *The Fifty-first Yearbook of the National Society for the Study of Education, Part I: General Education* (Chicago: University of Chicago Press, 1952), p. 13.

[11] Bestor, p. 403.

[12] David Riesman, "Some Observations on the 'Older' and the 'Newer' Social Sciences," in White, p. 323.

[13] McConnell, p. 13. See also *General Education in a Free Society* (Cambridge, Mass.: Harvard University Press, 1945).

tempt to adapt to American practice some counterpart of the Oxford and Cambridge tutorial system.[14]

Debate over the best possible curriculum is quite clearly one of the constant features of an ever-changing educational scene. Whether someone proposes that students study more or less science, classical or modern languages, seven liberal arts or seventy, there is sure to be a long and continuing controversy. Faculties are notorious for self-criticism and soul-searching, but the criticism and search, although animated in part by academic politics, also call forth a high order of speculation within the Renaissance tradition of discovery and investigation. And most important, the ideal to which all faculties in free societies aspire, is the ideal of the Renaissance: to fashion a man fit to live in freedom.

It is not surprising that the debate has been continual since the earliest university days, because the road that leads toward the ideal is difficult, often blocked by landslides in unsuspected places, and poses ever new challenges for professorial guides seeking the best way to traverse it. Students must also find their way along the road, ignoring the diversionary byways and avoiding the many hazards en route. They must learn much before they earn the right to rest at any of the way stations, and they have to acquire many skills in order to make the journey successfully.

The skills of the mind so necessary to a free man are not easy to acquire. Enlarging and disciplining one's powers is no sinecure. A student has a difficult task before him in learning to remember, to calculate, to measure, to manipulate, and to communicate with others, but he must do so nonetheless. And as he becomes more competent in these techniques, he must also learn the difficult art of making decisions and of choosing among alternatives of action and thought, for freedom implies choice, and

[14] See, for example, Shannon McCune *et al.*, *The New College Plan: A Proposal for a Major Departure in Higher Education* (Amherst, 1958); and W. Max Wise, *They Come for the Best of Reasons: College Students Today* (Washington: American Council on Education, 1958), pp. 43–45.

he who would be free must know how to question the *status quo*. If he accepts situations as they are, if without doubting he endorses another's way of doing or thinking, he denies all possibility of change. He must therefore learn to investigate all ideas, all procedures, all systems, all ways of thinking and doing, lest he impair his own freedom.

In addition to learning to think critically and not to accept authority blindly, he must develop his own values and learn to appreciate the values of others. He must cherish imagination, creative thought, and reason. He must love the truth and pursue it disinterestedly. He must come to understand why social scientists have to observe the world around them untrammeled by doctrinaire philosophies; why the humanists must be free to express themselves in the arts, literature, and music; why scientists should pry loose the secrets of the universe; why without those who are restless in the presence of the unknown, who have a passion for discovery and are eager to enrich the world with their knowledge, he cannot progress and will not be free.

What is more, he himself must learn the facts of the physical and social world around him, and the value of literature, art, and music. But since the facts he may have to work with tomorrow will in all likelihood differ from those available to him today, he must study not only what there is to know at the moment but also how, in the future, to gain knowledge. As John Henry Cardinal Newman put it more than a hundred years ago,

It [a liberal education] gives a man a clear conscious view of his own opinions and judgments, a truth in developing them, an eloquence in expressing them, and a force in urging them. It teaches him to see things as they are, to go right to the point, to disentangle a skein of thought, to detect what is sophistical, and to discard what is irrelevant. It prepares him to fill any post with credit and to master any subject with facility.[15]

15 *The Idea of a University* (1852), Discourse VII, sec. 10. For a fuller discussion of liberal education, see the following works on which the preceding three paragraphs are based: Robert N. Beck, "Let Us Liberalize Liberal Education," *School and Society*, LXXVII (Jan. 3, 1953), p. 4; Bestor, pp. 38, 395–97;

No one expects the student to face this responsibility alone. The teacher is there to help him along the road toward the ideals of freedom, but he too has heavy responsibilities. He must know his subject well, of course, but, beyond that, how he teaches is just as important as what he teaches. Pursuing truth, he cannot be dogmatic. His interpretation of history, literature, or science is, after all, just one interpretation, his own or another's, and it is not, in all likelihood, the only tenable interpretation. He cannot, therefore, give the student merely the central facts or ideals of any particular discipline; he must expose him to at least some of the raw materials from which he derives his own interpretations. He is obliged to encourage the student to examine the data (be they historical, literary, social, or scientific) and urge him to fashion his own hypotheses, to come to his own conclusions, and to test them by all appropriate techniques.

The faculty member by these means helps his students approach the Renaissance ideal, and, difficult though the task is, the prize is worth the pains, for if a faculty succeeds, its graduates will be able to carry the burden of freedom. They will be aware that there is usually more than one aspect to every problem. They will be willing and eager to hear all sides, and they will go along whatever avenue of life they may choose with questioning minds and an ingrained habit of not taking for granted what they are told. That the holders of the B.A. degree should be thinking persons is far more important than what they know or think at graduation.

It follows then that the free man must learn a method he can apply in circumstances neither he nor his professors can foresee exactly. Acquiring a liberal education, therefore, is a matter of preparing oneself to face an unknown future intelligently through

---

Gordon Keith Chalmers, "The Break in Liberalism," and Edmund E. Day, "Notes on the Reorientation of Liberal Education," in Association of American Colleges, *Bulletin*, XXXII (1946), 344, 385; Mark Van Doren, *Liberal Education* (New York: Henry Holt & Co., 1943), pp. 79, 144–45; Green, pp. 37–39; Harold Taylor, "The Aims of Education," *College English*, XVIII (1957), 246.

a curriculum which changes from age to age as the requirements of free men vary, and educators today must adapt their curricula to accommodate the changes which have occurred in society since the Renaissance scholars first enunciated their ideal. Today's graduates of colleges in the United States, unlike their counterparts in the twelfth century, do not go out into a primarily agricultural world to live as an educated class separated by wide gulfs from the common man. No longer are the majority of people rude, hard-working agricultural laborers, rarely leaving their land, unable to read, depending upon pilgrims and merchants for all they hear of the wider world.[16]

Compared with peoples before the Industrial Revolution or even peoples in our own time who live in underdeveloped lands, Americans can pursue higher education quite easily, even though they may still have to sacrifice time and money. In the future, higher standards of living and larger scholarship funds hold promise of taking even the dollar sign out of the picture. But Americans already enjoy leisure time which in other societies has been available only to aristocrats. With annual vacations, maximum hours of work and minimum wages largely set by law, and the fruits of mechanization and automation available to all, Americans have more time for themselves than any people on earth. Never have so many enjoyed so much for so long. How to spend great amounts of leisure time was once a problem only for Roman emperors. One may hope that today's Americans will be able to do better with it than Emperor Domitian, who was driven by boredom to pass his hours in killing flies.[17]

The qualities once important only for the freemen of Athens, the leaders of medieval society, and the privileged few in succeeding centuries, are now important for all the people and certainly for our college alumni. Invested with the suffrage, all those who

[16] John Herman Randall, Jr., *The Making of the Modern Mind* (Boston: Houghton Mifflin Co., 1940), p. 21.
[17] Woodward, p. 104.

inherit the mantle and responsibilities of freedom in modern times need the intelligence, initiative, wisdom, individualism, self-reliance, and cooperative understanding a liberal education provides. It is not merely the aristocrat today but all citizens who must know how to cultivate those arts most conducive to personal and national well-being.

Today's colleges and universities should be temperamentally attuned to broadening the outlook of students, for universities were among the first international institutions in the world. In the twelfth century, it was customary for students to travel to university centers in all parts of Europe to find wisdom wherever it was available.[18] The modern student is more fortunate than his medieval forebear, for with improved communications, most of the world's ideas are common currency, and free educational institutions have always cultivated contacts across political frontiers. One need only compare the greatness of the German universities in the nineteenth century with their disintegration under Hitler to realize how important it is, especially in the modern world, for a college or university to look outward as far as possible. Faculties and students who today open their minds to the ideas of the whole world and study the relations between their country and others serve simultaneously their own best interest and that of the nation, for living, as they do, in a world united by technology if not by politics, they are all affected by ideas and actions originating beyond the nation's frontiers.

Just how colleges and universities in the United States expose their students to the ways of the world varies somewhat from college to college, for in the United States, the spectrum of higher education is extraordinarily wide. Statistics do not by themselves reveal all its colors, but they do at least give some sense of its variety. In 1954–55 the United States accommodated 1,855 colleges and universities, 1,410 of which offered the bachelor's de-

[18] Hastings Rashdall, *The Universities of Europe in the Middle Ages* (Oxford: Clarendon Press, 1936), pp. 6–7.

gree in a liberal arts program. Of these liberal arts curricula, just over half (732) exist in colleges operating outside a university and offering no other educational plan, and 302 are available in colleges within universities. The remaining institutions award the B.A. or B.S. degrees but also enroll students in terminal programs and in curricula that specifically train them for the teaching or other professions.

Despite their large number, American colleges display certain common educational patterns. To summarize briefly: Most of them arrange their liberal arts programs in a four-year sequence. During the first two years, they require their students to take certain courses in the principal fields of knowledge, either surveys or interdisciplinary general education courses. At the start of the student's third year in most of these institutions, he picks a field of concentration or major, and, with the aid of a faculty adviser, arranges his program for the remainder of his college career at the rate of three to six courses per year. Some institutions distinguish the first two years of work from the last two by grouping them in junior and senior divisions or colleges and even providing separate administrative officers for the two categories. Sometimes they allow students to begin their professional studies in their third or fourth undergraduate year and receive both their bachelor and first professional degrees by the time they complete their training.

Although most American colleges adhere to this general outline, a few vary significantly from it in their programming, curriculum content, and method. Hiram College, for example, has a single-course plan, where students study one course at a time for each of five seven-week terms throughout each college year. St. John's College (Maryland) adheres to a curriculum based on a number of "great books" in various fields. Antioch College intersperses periods of study with periods of employment, thus giving students practical working experiences and opportunities to defray college expenses. Some colleges are now experimenting with individualized study programs, allowing their students to proceed toward their degrees rather more independently than in the past, fulfilling formal requirements through tutorial work and centrally administered examinations.

Despite innumerable variations in detail, however, all American institutions of higher learning tend more toward the English tradition of a resident college of students and teachers, rather than toward the Continental university plan. This collegiate pattern, most pronounced at the independent liberal arts institutions, brings students and faculty together in a community, and, where possible, provides facilities for them to meet not only formally but informally as well. The college idea owes a great deal to the Oxford and Cambridge patterns of university life, as opposed to those of the Continent, although the four-year program of liberal education is peculiarly American.

All these institutions, college or university, independent or state-financed, urban, suburban, or rural, like their counterparts in Europe and their predecessors going back to the Middle Ages, have to face the pressures of their own times and the need to fashion a curriculum meaningful to their own society. Today, all liberal arts college instructors have some responsibility for making their students aware of the interdependent world to which they belong. Even as faculty members share the responsibility of helping their students think and communicate effectively, make relevant judgments, and discriminate among values, so, too, do they share the burden of giving to their students the widest perspectives possible. They may broaden the outlook of their students on world affairs by offering in the curriculum specific courses concentrating on world affairs. Certainly there is a place for such courses in a college program, but since no aspect of the arts or sciences is free of influences from outside the United States, world affairs impinge on so many parts of the curriculum that no one course or department can by itself instruct students in them. In teaching about world affairs, therefore, faculties must do more than include specific courses in the curriculum. They must also recognize that professors in the humanities and the natural sciences, as well as the social sciences, have important responsibilities which are so far only partly realized in many of our colleges and universities. By examining each of these three areas of learning in turn, we can perhaps come to appreciate more fully the relation between each of them and world affairs.

# CHAPTER THREE

# Humanities, History, and World Affairs

> Art is a human activity having for its purpose the trans-
> mission to others of the highest and best feelings to which
> men have risen.
>
> L. N. TOLSTOI, *What Is Art?*

IT IS PERHAPS MOST LOGICAL to start our survey of what the several branches of the curriculum have to contribute to an understanding of world affairs with the humanities because they
embrace the oldest studies in the university. Like all the liberal
arts, the humanities help to develop the whole man and especially help man understand his inner aspirations and ideals.[1]
The studies that make up the humanities (literature, language,
philosophy, fine arts, music, as well as the broad, interdisciplinary courses embracing several of these subjects) show students the
hidden beauty of the world and the ideals existing beyond reality. The humanities give students some sense of belonging to a
tradition, allow them to participate in the great conversations of
the world, and enable them to share aesthetic experiences. They
awaken and enlarge the mind by making it the receptacle of a
thousand combinations of thought and feeling. They help a man
try to be, in Shelley's words, "greatly good" by enabling him to
"imagine intensely and comprehensively" and to put himself in

---

[1] *General Education in a Free Society* (Cambridge, Mass.: Harvard University Press, 1945), p. 59.

the place of many others; through the humanities "the pains and pleasures of his species" become his own.[2]

## *Literature*

Conventionally, most American colleges introduce students to the humanities through survey courses in English or American literature, but there is a growing awareness that such courses do not take advantage of all the excellent possibilities inherent in the humanities. They do not put students in touch with the feelings, aspirations, hopes, and thoughts of most of the world, and they unnecessarily cut most American students off from the great literatures outside the Anglo-Saxon tradition.

One of the first professors to realize this deficiency was John Erskine, who undertook his "great books" seminar for upperclassmen at Columbia College after World War I. Erskine brought students into direct contact with the great minds and great literature of our culture, and others followed his example in similar courses at Reed College and the Experimental College at the University of Wisconsin (under Alexander Meiklejohn) in the 1920's, and at the University of Chicago and St. John's College in the 1930's. Despite these innovations most colleges continued through World War II to introduce students to literature in more conventional ways. Very often faculties designed these beginning courses primarily for the future specialists and only secondarily for the student taking but one course in literature. There is every reason in the world for tomorrow's professor of English literature to study everything from Beowulf to Virginia Woolf or T. S. Eliot but, except for the specialist, the chronological view of the successive stages of English literature, illustrated by selections from a two-volume anthology, has not much to recommend it. The nonspecialist would certainly obtain a truer picture of mankind's literary achievements if his reading went

---

[2] Harry Buxton Forman (ed.), *The Prose Works of Percy Bysshe Shelley* (London: Reeves & Turner, 1880), III, 111.

beyond English and American literature. Such, at least, was the feeling at Indiana University, where the course in literature has an interesting history. A "world literature" course first appeared at the university in 1925 as a "service" course for the School of Business. Gradually, however, all parts of the university accepted it, first as an alternative to existing courses in English literature, and then, in place of the English literature survey, as the only introductory course. Its range is shown by the authors whose works are often included: Homer, Sophocles, Chaucer, Dante, Shakespeare, Swift, Voltaire, Dostoevski, and Hawthorne.[3]

Inspired by the general education movement, more and more faculties have attempted not only to help the student who will not specialize in literature to understand his cultural heritage but also to give him some perspective about it. For instance, they have transmuted comprehensive surveys of American or English literature into courses which concentrate on major works of important cultural periods in the history of Western civilization: the Periclean Age, the Middle Ages, the Renaissance, the Reformation, the Age of Enlightenment, and modern times. The assignments are important for their literary quality and for philosophical content. For instance, the students read some of the works (in translation, where necessary) of Homer, Plato, Sophocles, the Bible, Chaucer, Dante, Shakespeare, Descartes, and Voltaire. Haverford College's Interpretations of Life in Western Literature is a course of this type, incuding not only the older classics but more recent works with intrinsic merit, such as Renan's Life of Jesus and Koestler's Darkness at Noon.[4]

At Wesleyan University, the students read portions of the Bible, and works by Aeschylus, Sophocles, Euripides, Aristotle, Plato, Marcus Aurelius, Dante, Luther, Bunyan, Montaigne,

---

[3] Philip B. Daghlian and Horst Frenz, "Evolution of a World Literature Course," College English, XII (1950), 150–53.

[4] J. Glenn Gray, "The Humanities at Haverford College," in Earl J. McGrath (ed.), The Humanities in General Education (Dubuque, Iowa: William C. Brown Co., 1949), pp. 1–14.

Marlowe, Shakespeare, Descartes, Voltaire, Goethe, Mill, and Whitehead. The Wesleyan course places more emphasis on religion than the Haverford course.[5] An elective course in the humanities at Wesleyan which follows the first one includes Greek, medieval, and Renaissance art and music and the art and music of the eighteenth, nineteenth, and twentieth centuries as well as works by Homer, Aristotle, Chaucer, Shakespeare, Pascal, Leibniz, Voltaire, Whitehead, Dostoevski, Ibsen, and Saint Exupéry.[6] Similar courses exist now across the country.

A number of institutions—for instance, the University of Chicago, Chatham College, and Stephens College—prefer to have students understand and appreciate the arts themselves rather than their cultural or philosophical significance. Courses at these colleges focus attention on the art objects, whether drawn from painting, sculpture, architecture, music, poetry, drama, or the dance. The instructors use audio-visual aids of all kinds and place much more emphasis on analyzing the work of art and on discovering the principles and techniques underlying the creative process than do the instructors in courses using the historical, cultural, or philosophical approach.[7]

In all these courses, it is clear that teachers of the humanities have made formidable strides in recent years toward meeting the needs of the modern general student. They are helping today's degree candidates understand more than the cultural background of England or America by exploring with them frontiers extending backward in time to ancient Greece and eastward in distance to prerevolutionary Russia. Still other frontiers remain, however, in the Middle and Far East and Southeast Asia, for the humanists to cross in educating the general student. Almost

---

[5] Norman O. Brown, "The Humanities at Wesleyan University," in *ibid.*, pp. 30–41.

[6] *Loc. cit.*

[7] See Robert F. Davidson, "Trends in General Education in the Humanities," in *ibid.*, p. 297, as well as descriptive chapters by the several contributors to the volume.

without exception, the courses offered in the humanities today deal primarily with the Western cultural tradition and largely ignore the non-Western world.[8]

The reasons for the prevailing patterns are both philosophical and practical. Philosophically, one may justify limiting courses in the humanities to the Western cultural areas because American students will live for the most part in a Western cultural tradition.[9] It is part of their heritage, and they must know about it. However, Americans in this and the next century will have increasing contact with non-Western peoples with rich cultural heritages of their own in China, India, Japan, Africa, and the Arab world. Ideally, therefore, courses in literature, art, and philosophy should also expose students to non-Western cultures.

The practical problems Westerners face in studying these cultures are admittedly vast, especially for instructors who eschew texts and anthologies. For those who would intensify the students' experience by bringing them in contact with whole works or large portions of works, selecting readings or finding time to offer all the nonliterary material one must present in broad, cultural courses is far more difficult than merely assigning pages in an anthology. Having left the well-trod path of English literature, humanities staffs already face formidable problems in choosing alternate byways even within Western cultural fields. The readings, lectures, and discussion programs in most of the present courses cannot help being overcrowded; they cannot otherwise treat Greek, Roman, Renaissance, English, American, and Continental literatures, art, or philosophy. To extend the curriculum to include the cultural contributions of the rest of the world is obviously troublesome.

[8] For comments on this subject, see John D. Kendall, "General Education: Humanities," in *Current Issues in Higher Education* (Washington: Association for Higher Education, 1956), p. 208. For an interesting exception, see chap. 9, *infra*.

[9] See, for example, the remarks of John S. Kieffer, "The Humanities in St. John's Program," in McGrath, *Humanities*, p. 44.

Courses in Western literatures make considerable demands on teachers, requiring them to engage in extensive programs of self-education. These demands are as nothing, however, compared with those which courses including Far Eastern and Southeast Asian materials make upon instructors. All teachers of literature, after all, have read the *Odyssey* before, and either have the classical background or know how to acquire it. Even Russian materials in translation have become much more accessible in recent years, and the works of Tolstoi, Turgenev, and Dostoevski have long been discussed and analyzed by English-speaking and -writing critics. But teachers need assistance even to begin considering such works as the Babylonian legend of Gilgamesh; the Indian *Panchatantra, Bhagavad-Gita,* and *Sakuntala;* and the Japanese *Tale of Genji.* It would most certainly be desirable to include in humanities courses literary, artistic, and philosophical works from the Russian, Indian, and Chinese cultures, but before faculties can even begin to adjust their curricula to do so, they must have available the materials needed to teach the works they select. Providing texts, commentaries, and bibliographies has offered excellent opportunities for cooperative scholarly ventures by Unesco, private publishers, and foundations and learned societies interested in encouraging the teaching of the humanities and in promoting an interest in Middle Eastern, Far Eastern, and Southeast Asian cultures. Public and private support to intensify these efforts is essential.[10]

[10] George L. Anderson has made an excellent analysis of the problem of making materials available and suggested some excellent approaches to it in "Cathay and the Way Thither: Oriental Literature in the World Literature Program," *Modern Language Journal,* XL (1956), 316–18. See also Hazel Stewart Allerson, "The Significance of World Literature Today," *College English,* VII (1946), 323–26; George B. de Huszar, "The Classics and International Understanding," *Learning and World Peace* (New York: Harper & Bros., 1948), pp. 200–219; John D. Kendall, "General Education: Humanities," *Current Issues in Higher Education* (1956), p. 208. See also John D. Yohannan (ed.), *A Treasury of Asian Literature* (New York: John Day Co., 1956); inexpensive translations made available by Twayne Publishers and the Grove Press; and the *Yearbook of Comparative and General Literature* (Chapel Hill: University

Only by making extraordinary efforts to broaden still further our approaches to diverse world cultures can we make our humanities courses entirely suitable for the twentieth century, where the very insights that literary and artistic masterpieces can provide are essential to help the contemporary citizen understand other peoples. These same efforts, of course, would make it increasingly possible to expand the advanced course offerings in non-Western literatures, which, as electives, would be very valuable to those students whose interest in these cultures was awakened by the required programs.

In addition to broadening the content of literature courses, there are possibilities even in teaching the English language of widening the students' contacts with the world at large. In composition courses, either for freshmen or advanced students, instructors assign not only writing projects but also readings in works chosen to illustrate diverse literary styles. In selecting this reading, instructors have unlimited possibilities of enlarging students' cultural horizons, for they can include literary works from the traditions of various countries or use materials on world affairs among the nonfiction reading assignments.

It is even possible to base an entire composition course on world affairs, as, for instance, one instructor at Colby Junior College did just after the war; while teaching the mechanics of English, she introduced students to the areas of the world about which they knew least. The students read pamphlets giving them some idea of the land, people, and politics of the Far East, Africa, or Latin America. Then they read novels, short stories, and poetry representing the areas. The reading also included controversial political material; and through reports, class discussions, short papers, and research projects the students learned a great deal about world affairs in a course designed primarily

---

of North Carolina [annual]). For an account of Unesco's work, see *Proposed Programme and Budget for 1957–1958* (Paris: Unesco, 1956), pp. 127–28.

to equip them with the mechanics of the English language.[11] Such a program should commend itself to others, especially in small colleges where the possibilities of offering elaborate programs in world affairs are limited.

Other opportunities for enhancing instruction in world affairs exist in courses in English composition. In fact, in these freshman English courses, colleges have only begun to create the fruitful cooperation among faculty members in the various disciplines which holds promise of giving the general student the kind of training he needs. At Colgate University, for instance, where there is no formal course in freshman English, a most interesting development has occurred. The university has arranged for the English Department to work out assignments for freshman term papers together with all other departments offering courses to freshmen. The instructors choose the topics for papers they assign in their own courses, but the English Department sees that the freshman assignments throughout the year include all types of writing conventionally included in college composition courses, from outlines and précis to research papers. Both the instructors in whose courses the papers are assigned and an instructor in English grade the students' papers. The English instructor then continues to work with the individual student in correcting and improving his work.[12] This program not only increases the impact the instruction in English composition has on students, but it relates the work in English to that in other fields; it also provides the instructors in social science with an opportunity to require more written work of their students than they might otherwise. Consequently, it increases the possibilities for students interested in world affairs to indulge their interests.

Even in conventional courses in English composition, however, instructors should be sure to point out that many government

---

[11] Signi Falk, "International Understanding: An Experiment in Freshman English," *College English*, VIII (1947), 196–203.

[12] S. Lawson, "Colgate Plan for Improving Student Writing," Association of American Colleges, *Bulletin*, XXXIX (1953), 288–90.

agencies and officials of the United Nations believe students of public affairs can receive no training so important as that of preparing the reports which are the lifeblood of any bureaucracy. All major governments are concerned about the bad writing which impedes their business.[13] What is more, language is extremely important in conducting foreign relations and diplomacy,[14] a point which all teachers of English composition can emphasize by drawing their students' attention to readily obtainable materials on world affairs: state papers, speeches of prominent officials of the Department of State or of foreign ministries, transcripts of press conferences, and the texts of treaties. All these writings provide excellent examples of how important it is in conducting world affairs to draft documents carefully, to use language precisely, to be alert for every possible shade of meaning, and to avoid misstatement which may have grave consequences. Analyzing newspapers to illustrate the diverse ways they cover foreign news stories is also a most informative and revealing exercise.

## Foreign Languages

Next to English, foreign languages are among the most important of the subjects in the humanities because they provide students with many keys to understanding man and his works. They are obviously important to students of world affairs. Colleges are still far from realizing the potential contribution foreign languages can make to the education of a liberal arts student, however, because the American primary and secondary schools do not emphasize foreign languages sufficiently. Ideally, most

[13] See, for instance, C. Dale Fuller, *Training of Specialists in International Relations* (Washington: American Council on Education, 1957), pp. 50–51, 94–96, 100, 102, 115, 120; Sir Ernest Gowers, *The Complete Plain Words* (London: Her Majesty's Stationery Office, 1954); André Moufflet, "Le Langage de l'Administration et sa psychologie," *Vie et Langage*, No. 55 (October 1956), pp. 471–75, and *Plain Letters* (Washington: Government Printing Office, 1955).

[14] See, for example, "Diplomatic Language," in Harold Nicolson, *Diplomacy* (London: Oxford University Press, 1950).

American students going to college would, like their counterparts in Europe, work hard at foreign languages before they came to a college or university. If students really knew one foreign language when they were graduated from high schools, college language instructors could revolutionize their teaching. Instead of drilling students in the rudiments, they would be free to share with them intellectual experiences which have been an integral part of the humanistic tradition in Western universities since the Middle Ages. They would be able to help students take what the Harvard Report called "a Copernican step, one of the most liberating, the most exciting, and the most sobering opportunities for reflection that the humanities can offer."[15] They would give their students some perspective about the English language and about American culture; acquaint them with the limits language imposes on individual and national thinking; help them to tear down stereotypes; and assist them to appreciate foreign cultures.[16]

College language teaching in the United States today, however, is in general far more rudimentary because so few students master a foreign language before college. Although more primary schools than ever before are teaching foreign languages, they are not numerous.[17] Moreover, many high schools either do not

---

[15] P. 120.

[16] An effective case for teaching foreign languages is made by William R. Parker, "Why a Foreign Language Requirement?" *College and University,* XXXIII (Winter 1957), 189–203; see also "Modern Language Teaching and Intercultural Understanding," in "FL Bulletin" (Mimeographed; New York: Modern Language Association of America, 1955); Marjorie C. Johnston, "How Can Modern Language Teaching Promote International Understanding?" in National Association of Secondary-School Principals, *Bulletin,* XL (1956), 70; Henri Peyre, "The Need for Language Study in America Today," *Modern Language Journal,* XL (1956), 326; Henry Grattan Doyle, "Will Translation Suffice?" Language Leaflet No. 10 (Washington: George Washington University, 1940).

[17] In 1940, fewer than 5,000 grade school pupils studied foreign languages, but in September 1955, 271,617 children in 1,977 public elementary schools in 357 cities and towns in the United States received foreign language instruction from their classroom teachers or from visiting language teachers, and the figures represented an increase of 62,000 pupils in one year. See *The*

teach foreign languages or require them for graduation;[18] and whereas in 1922, 70 percent of our colleges required students to offer modern languages for admission, only 28 percent do today.[19] Traditional objections to language training—that it is superfluous, that students do not retain their skill, and that the teaching is poor—combined with American political and cultural isolationism to bring language instruction from a World War I peak to an all-time low just before World War II. The result was a paradox: during the eighteenth and nineteenth centuries, without cables, telephone, radio, steamships, planes, and movies, every well-educated man in the United States knew foreign languages; but in this century, with all the marvels of communication, vast numbers of educated Americans were left culturally isolated, linguistically at sea.[20]

World War II did a good deal to revive interest in foreign languages. Many returning soldiers had a natural desire to study languages which their experiences overseas had shown them to be worthwhile or necessary. The war also stimulated their concern and the concern of other Americans for foreign peoples. The United States Armed Forces themselves encouraged an inter-

---

*FL Program,* Report No. 3 (New York: Modern Language Association of America, 1956), p. 3; see also Kenneth W. Mildenberger, *Status of Foreign Language Study in American Elementary Schools in 1955* (Washington: Office of Education, Department of Health, Education, and Welfare, 1955); Ed Kiester, "Foreign Languages in Grade School," *Parade,* Sept. 9, 1956, pp. 9–13; "Experiment in Language Teaching," *New York Times,* Feb. 16, 1958, p. E9; and U.S. Office of Education, *Modern Foreign Languages in the High School* (Washington: Government Printing Office, 1958).

[18] In the United States 56 percent of the public high schools do not even offer courses in modern foreign languages; only about 14 percent of all public high schools enroll students in any kind of modern foreign language class. "Foreign Language Entrance and Degree Requirements," *PMLA,* LXX (September 1955), Part 2, 52–56; "FL Program Notes," *PMLA,* LXXII (June 1957), ix; and "Foreign Language Entrance and Degree Requirements for the B.A. Degree," *PMLA,* LXXII (September 1957), Part 2, 33.

[19] "Foreign Language Entrance and Degree Requirements," *PMLA,* LXVIII (September 1953), Part 2, 40; and *ibid.,* LXXII (September 1957), Part 2, 33.

[20] J. Allen Pfeffer, "Modern Languages in the American College Curriculum," *Modern Language Journal,* XXXIX (1955), 64.

est in foreign languages. Finding themselves woefully short of personnel competent to deal directly with the many non-English-speaking peoples with whom the global war effort brought them in contact, they established schools of their own during the war, where they taught languages with great success to students who had the maximum incentive. As recently as 1958, President Eisenhower called attention to the need for the government to help refurbish language teaching in the United States because of American global responsibilities,[21] and Congress responded by passing the National Defense Education Act of 1958 (PL 85–864), which in Title VI authorizes funds for improving language teaching throughout the nation.

How desperately the United States needs to encourage people to study languages is clear to all who know that, in 1958, 50 percent of the Foreign Service officer corps did not have a speaking knowledge of any foreign language and that 70 percent of the new men coming into the Service were in the same predicament.[22]

As a result of this new awareness of the importance and value of foreign languages, colleges began to reassess their curricula, and in recent years the institutions have been reversing the interwar trend of abandoning foreign language requirements for graduation.[23] The following tabulation shows the number of institutions which in 1954–55 were offering instruction in languages:[23]

[21] See President's Message on Education, 85th Cong., 2d Sess., H. Doc. 318, *Congressional Record,* CIV (1958), 923–24.

[22] James Reston, "Foreign Service Woes," *New York Times,* March 19, 1958, p. 14.

[23] *The FL Program,* Report Nos. 1 and 3 (New York:Modern Language Association of America, 1954 and 1956); "Foreign Language Entrance and Degree Requirements for the B.A. Degree," *PMLA,* LXXII (September 1957), Part 2, 33. At present, of 840 accredited colleges and universities offering the B.A. degree, 704 (83.9 percent) require all students seeking the bachelor's degree to study a foreign language. According to a survey of 971 institutions made in 1954–55, 60 modern foreign languages are available in American colleges today. As the accompanying tabulation shows. French is the most readily available, with Spanish and German ranking second and third. At least 493 institutions offer all three of these languages.

The institutions offering a considerable number of the languages previously

| Language | No. of Institutions | Language | No. of Institutions |
|---|---|---|---|
| French | 905 | Romanian | 7 |
| Spanish | 867 | Danish | 6 |
| German | 825 | Modern Greek | 6 |
| Italian | 212 | Bulgarian | 5 |
| Russian | 183 | Hungarian | 5 |
| Portuguese | 69 | Ukrainian | 5 |
| Hebrew | 47 | Armenian | 4 |
| Chinese | 36 | Dutch | 4 |
| Japanese | 24 | Hindu | 4 |
| Polish | 23 | Indonesian | 4 |
| Swedish | 23 | Mongolian | 4 |
| Norwegian | 18 | Thai | 3 |
| Arabic | 13 | Vietnamese | 3 |
| Turkish | 11 | Slovak | 2 |
| Persian | 10 | Tagalog | 2 |
| Czech | 8 | Tibetan | 2 |
| Korean | 8 | Urdu | 2 |
| Serbo-Croation | 8 | | |

The war affected not only the language offerings, but also the methods of teaching languages. Colleges have profited from the experience of the Armed Forces in emphasizing speech and oral-aural approaches. Many of the claims on behalf of the methods of the Armed Forces are exaggerated, but they did shake up traditional college language instruction in many desirable ways. Numerous colleges now emphasize the spoken language; use "language laboratories" with recording equipment and other

---

considered exotic are Columbia, California, Yale, Georgetown, Harvard, Washington, Cornell, and Indiana. For a complete list see *PMLA*, LXIX, Supplement (September 1954), 26–33; see also "Foreign Language Entrance and Degree Requirements," *PMLA*, LXXI (September 1956), Part 2, 49–70; and William R. Parker, "Why a Foreign Language Requirement?" *College and University*, XXXIII (Winter 1957), 189–203. On a national basis there is obviously an impressive reservoir of instruction in modern foreign languages in our colleges and universities. But the statistics also indicate some great educational deserts and leave no room for complacency. See testimony of Frederick Burkhardt for the American Council of Learned Societies, before the Senate Labor and Public Welfare Committee, as reported in the *New York Times*, March 16, 1958, p. 60, and *American Students Abroad: Goodwill Ambassadors* (Syracuse, N.Y.: Maxwell Graduate School of Citizenship and Public Affairs, Syracuse University, 1958), p. 4.

aids to learning, pronunciation, and speech; and employ drill periods to supplement regular instruction.

Cornell University has been in the vanguard in developing and applying many of the oral-aural techniques, and other colleges have altered their curricula to include the new methods. Michigan State University offers both traditional and conversational work in languages; the University of Michigan also conducts special conversation classes; the University of Illinois enrolls a majority of its students in traditional courses, but also has intensive courses using oral-aural methods, and then puts both groups into a third semester reading course, with good results; Harvard tries to teach reading, writing, understanding, and speaking in intensive courses using an eclectic approach; and the University of California offers both regular and intensive work in language. Other colleges retain the conventional language programs and add optional laboratory periods for those students who desire them with additional credit (University of Rochester) or without credit as a service for students (Brooklyn College). Princeton and the University of Colorado have tried and abandoned the new methods, believing that they emphasize the "tool" aspects of the language above the humanistic insights of literature, creative imagination, and poetic wisdom, which, they maintain, colleges should not sacrifice to conversations on the "gastronomic, the athletic, or itinerary."[24] Experiments nonetheless go forward in teaching foreign languages, and will undoubtedly continue to do so at an increasing pace under the stimulus of federal funds.

The opportunities in language courses to convey to students more than the code of a language and to incorporate teaching related to world affairs are great indeed. Some instructors have for a long time leavened language instruction by introducing into their elementary courses the materials of art, history, government, or literature. Many have used maps effectively in their

[24] Pfeffer, pp. 64–68.

classes and managed to convey some idea of the regional and topographical patterns within a country. Some have turned their courses into miniature area studies programs by discussing (in English, if necessary) topographical, political, economic, and demographic problems; political structure, mores, patterns, foreign relations; and geography and how it has influenced the history, culture, and economics of non-English-speaking countries. Some instructors have begun their courses with a few lectures along these lines and have interspersed additional ones throughout the semester,[25] bringing in visiting specialists if necessary.

All these efforts are commendable, but a great deal more still remains to be done. How much language teachers can do to convey the idea of a foreign culture has been suggested in a very significant seminar held in 1953 by the Modern Language Association.[26] The report points out that language teachers have always argued that "foreign languages are not only useful but necessary for an understanding of other peoples and other cultures."[27] Too often, however, the report concludes, language teachers equate culture exclusively with "the enlightenment and refinement of taste acquired by intellectual and aesthetic training" and "that which is admirable, superior or desirable." Only rarely do they regard culture in the broader sociological sense of "the whole range of customary activities of the members of a society."[28] Foreign language elementary textbooks, for instance, often try to represent the culture through the writings of distinguished men of letters, but although the selections are primarily excellent as literature, they do not necessarily deal with other significant factors of contemporary culture. Other texts contain auxiliary nonliterary material, but they do not always pre-

[25] See Thomas W. Palmer, Jr., "An Area Approach for the Language Professor," *Modern Language Journal*, XL (1956), 31–33.

[26] "Developing Cultural Understanding through Foreign Language Study: A Report of the MLA Interdisciplinary Seminar in Language and Culture," *PMLA*, LXVIII (1953), 1196–1218.

[27] *Ibid.*, p. 1196.

[28] *Ibid.*, p. 1203.

sent a coherent picture of the culture. Still other texts are "cultural miscellanies," tending to be "altogether haphazard in their choice of subject matter." And some texts represent the facts of particular cultures in a "panoramic and encyclopedic" fashion, but they either tend to be propagandistic or else they do not make students aware of significant features and values in the foreign culture. All the texts, in short, "lack a sufficiently clear focus upon the relevant aspects of the foreign culture as contrasted with the student's own experience and value systems."[29]

The participants in the seminar drew the attention of language teachers to a vast array of sociological essays, describing patterns and themes in cultures and giving a well-rounded view of a people and its activities. The seminar suggested that language teachers, instead of presenting only literary materials, could find suitable reading for their students in accounts by native or foreign observers, periodical writing of an expository or argumentative nature, historical works, and travel literature.

In effect the MLA Interdisciplinary Seminar called upon language teachers to move from the first to the second idea of culture, a recommendation which has startled and offended many of them deeply. They object that the report takes the teaching of languages too far from the humanities and thus sacrifices some of its principal virtues. Rather than expose students to culture, it seems to urge language teachers to teach about culture.[30] On the other hand, since language teachers inevitably must teach about culture, there seems no reason to believe that they cannot, by broadening their approach to their subject, contribute even more than they do now to the intellectual leadership of their time.[31] In the past, few language students have ever grasped the

---

[29] *Ibid.*, p. 1202.

[30] Roosevelt University, incidentally, permits students to substitute a year's work in "culture studies" for a modern language.

[31] See Howard Lee Nostrand, "On Teaching a Foreign Culture," *Modern Language Journal*, XL (1956), 297–301.

cultural traditions of the country whose language they studied,[32] and the new proposals seem to offer some way of capturing this awareness for larger numbers of students.

The seminar challenged language teachers to change their own outlook, their professional training, and their teaching methods. It opened a Pandora's box by calling for a kind of "teacher of foreign language such as has rarely walked this planet."[33] Language teachers might have to become not simply

teachers of literature or linguistics temporarily arrested or frustrated permanently, in their growth into proper professors of literature or linguistics, but experts in their own peculiar right whose competence as teachers of foreign language depends upon a somewhat different, still rigorous, disciplined intellectual activity which has more direct application to the teaching of foreign language than either literature or linguistics.[34]

One can appreciate the kind of revolution such a change would entail by reflecting that it would mean that very highly trained teachers and not some young graduate student earning his way toward a Ph.D. would have to teach beginning language classes. It should still be possible for language teachers to present at an advanced level the courses in literature in the original language which in the past have been their principal delight. But by raising their sights, they might make the elementary courses both more interesting to themselves and more useful to the students. To contribute to a liberal arts education in the ways which the seminar report suggests, language teachers will need help from the social scientists to work out both the cultural materials which students should read in their language courses and to devise the kind of training best suited for language teachers who endorse this approach. Here is a fruitful field of cooperation between social scientists and humanists where so far they have done very little.

[32] *General Education in a Free Society*, p. 121.
[33] Charles E. Odegaard, "MLA Interdisciplinary Seminar on Language and Culture," *Modern Language Journal*, XXXVIII (1954), 167.
[34] *Ibid.*, p. 168.

## History

A more conventional link between the humanities and social sciences has already been forged by historians. History bridges the humanities and the social sciences because it is both an art and a science. It is an art because it is most important in what it suggests and connotes, and because it gives its readers understanding, wisdom, and experience. It makes its students widely traveled, as it were, and gives them perspective and a sense of time and change. As Thomas Fuller has said, "History maketh a young man to be old, without either wrinkles or gray hairs, privileging him with the experience of ages without either the infirmities or inconvenience thereof."[35] History thus helps students develop discrimination and a basis for judgments, which, while not final, may be imbued with wisdom. Like philosophers, the best of Clio's devotees bring ideas together, study problems, and interpret their causes. They use all the while social science, political and economic theory, statistics, psychology, art, and the behavioral sciences. They attempt to show the patterns and meanings of events and try to supply depth and perspective to complex problems.

History is, on the other hand, a science, for it attempts to be as exact as possible, using statistics, and checking contemporary data against the test of time. It examines the basic suppositions of the hypotheses of social science and tests them in the widest possible context, and at the same time it supplies the social scientists with data. Unlike social scientists, who usually examine only a segment of the human pageant, historians try to point out the complexity of man's activities, to interpret events in the face of multitudinous facts, and to supply depth and perspective to complex problems

[35] Quoted by William O. Aydelotte ("History in a Liberal Education," *Journal of General Education*, III [1948], 48), whose remarks together with those of Richard D. Challener and Maurice Lee, Jr. ("History and the Social Sciences: The Problem of Communications; Notes on a Conference Held by the Social Science Research Council," *American Historical Review*, LXII [1956], 331–38), have been most useful in preparing these paragraphs.

by painting on a large canvas. Historians can help expose over-simplified solutions to problems by drawing from the record of man's experience through time, and thus they help both beginning and advanced students develop critical standards.

The historian's mission since the time of Thucydides has been to present an exact knowledge of the past as an aid to interpreting the future.[36] The kind of aid that history gives the student of world affairs has, of course, often been misunderstood, and many people, even historians, have held quite unhistorical notions about history, some of which have been disastrous for everyone. Treitschke's view on German Destiny, for instance, so important in World Wars I and II, was based on historical "truths" which the rest of the world later had to put right, and much the same can be said for Marx's theory of economic determinism and Lenin's views of "the last stages of capitalism" which have colored so much thinking in the Soviet Union. Many ideas about wars need also be corrected: that wars are inevitable (a view shared by some groups on both sides of the iron curtain), that they relieve population pressures (which many aggressors have argued), or that they are justified for acquiring colonies or *Lebensraum*. The historian himself must wage a constant battle to put in proper perspective lessons badly learned from history,[37] for only the further study of history can cure unhistorical hallucinations.

Despite the constant danger that man may misinterpret history, he must contemplate events and movements of the past to understand world affairs today. The study of world affairs in fact is an offshoot of historical studies, so history continues to be one of the fields closest in spirit and content to world affairs. History provides information and perspective about the various encounters among

[36] "The Peloponnesian War," *The Complete Writings of Thucydides*, trans. Richard Crawley (New York: Modern Library, 1934), p. 14.

[37] For comments on the dangers of misinterpreting history, see J. G. Randall, "Historianship," *American Historical Review*, LVIII (1953), 249–64. For a striking example of differences among historians as to what is historical, see H. R. Trevor-Roper, "Arnold Toynbee's Millennium," *Encounter* (London), VIII (June 1957), 14–28.

nations and peoples, the economic and social factors that have influenced them, the struggle for tolerance and peace, all of which are the indispensable background for many contemporary issues.[38]

Many colleges continue to offer courses in European or American history as part of the program for the bachelor's degree because of their obvious value, although history now also appears in general education courses in the humanities and the social sciences. These arrangements reflect in part history's place in both areas of learning, attempts by faculties to establish connections among the various branches of knowledge, and the need to reduce to manageable proportions the continually growing accumulation of history for study.

Few of these courses realize their full potential to help students understand world affairs. American history courses are likely to be too provincial; humanities and social science courses run the danger of slurring history itself and thus ignoring the important ways in which history can help educate students; and scarcely any of the courses emphasize sufficiently the histories of Russia and the Far East, so important to Americans today.

In many American history courses, for instance, instructors tend to play down the influences of world events on the United States or of the United States on world events. Too often they treat tariff questions as though they affected merely sectional politics in the United States and not foreign countries. They frequently report British and French attitudes toward the Confederacy without explaining them, describe the Emancipation Proclamation without relating it to comparable humanitarian efforts elsewhere, or examine the American Revolution and the War of 1812 without connecting them to European colonialism or the Napoleonic wars.

American history instructors can give their courses a global aspect by helping students take sidelong glances at events off the

38 See P. O. Carr, "Approaches to the Study of World Affairs," *Middle States Council for the Social Studies, Proceedings* (1954), pp. 15–17.

main track of their study and thus keep them constantly aware of the wider world outside the United States. Just because American diplomatic history is often taught as a separate subject is no reason for students to slight the reciprocal influence of the United States and world affairs. For students of United States history not to appreciate the global significance of the Monroe Doctrine, the effect of American ideals on nations abroad, the role of the British Navy in securing our westward movement, or the impact of our Neutrality Acts on the rest of the world, would be most regrettable.

As important as it is for all Americans to study their own history, they should also know European history, which gives them insights into the motives and actions of other peoples with similar hopes and aspirations. European history always touches heavily on international relations, so that any student of European history is automatically something of a student of world affairs. European history courses do not always relate events in Europe to their consequences outside the Continent, however, and they would be more effective in developing a world view if they did. There are growing numbers of courses on United States history since 1865 or Europe in the twentieth century, and these are particularly valuable in introducing students to world affairs, although they should not displace courses which help students understand American or European history in depth,[39] so essential if they are to comprehend current problems. In fact, one can argue effectively in favor of exposing students to historical periods far removed from their own in order to give them the valuable experience of traveling great distances in time.[40] In any case, the two types of knowledge are not mutually exclusive.

Influenced by the general education movement, a number of

[39] See Charles E. Nowell, "Has the Past a Place in History?" *Journal of Modern History*, XXIV (1952), 331–40; George Barr Carson, Jr., "The Vanishing Historian," *AAUP Bulletin*, XXXIX (1953), 474–83.

[40] See D. C. Somervell, "History as a University Subject," *Universities Quarterly*, VII (1953), 147–50.

institutions are offering histories of civilization (or Western civilization). In these courses, students study about selected significant men, ideas, and events of their heritage. Sometimes these courses are surveys, differing only slightly from conventional instruction in European and American history, which chronicle systematically significant events from the fall of the Roman Empire down to the first (or second) World War. Those courses which most closely identify themselves with general education, however, concentrate on particular cultural epochs, and attempt to search out the "climate of opinion" or "ideal types," or to isolate in "typical" centuries an ideal type within them. For example, at Michigan State University, the History of Civilization course takes up the nature of civilization and depicts the civilization of Greece, Rome, the Middle Ages, the Renaissance and Reformation, the eighteenth century, the French Revolution and its aftermath, and the problems of contemporary civilization. The instructors do not attempt to supply a continuous chronological thread in this course, concentrating instead on giving an insight into the character of each era. The comparable course at Harvard College deals with fewer cultural epochs: Anglo-Saxon society, the thirteenth-century Church, the rise of Parliament, the Puritan Revolution, the age of Louis XIV, British reforms in the nineteenth century, Germany under Bismarck, and Marxian socialism.[41] A course of this type—one of the earliest—is Contemporary Civilization at Columbia. Instructors use a chronological and topical approach to ask, concerning the various periods of Western civilization since the Middle Ages, how men have made a living, how they have lived together, and how they have interpreted the world they live in. Instructors provide the students with a chronological framework by assigning secondary readings and supplemental material on political, economic, and philosophical

[41] See H. H. Kimber, "The Humanities in General Education at Michigan State College," in McGrath, *Humanities*, pp. 69–80; Samuel H. Beer, "Social Sciences 2 at Harvard," in Earl J. McGrath (ed.), *Social Science in General Education* (Dubuque, Iowa: William C. Brown Co., 1948), pp. 1–14.

developments in Western civilization. The staff hopes to capture "the best of history without history's narrowness or insularity."[42]

These courses, insofar as they search out general patterns of social behavior and lay down general laws for man, owe much to the social sciences, particularly social psychology, but they also draw upon the humanities by bringing in literature and philosophy. Some historians charge that in certain cases, instructors have, in bringing social science and literature into their courses, made history itself disappear from the curriculum. They do not believe that students are getting the data in the form of facts and chronology which the older history surveys provided. They allege that some of these courses impose a unity where none may in fact exist, leave students to infer a relation between environment and behavior which is not so clear as the courses imply, and that in seeking out typical people or centuries, the courses disrupt the sense of continuity and historical development which the older survey courses supply.[43] Whether critics may reasonably level this indictment at any individual course depends in large part on the instructor's approach and the details of the reading assignments. The danger of banishing history from the curriculum clearly exists if the history of civilization course concentrates primarily on literature and philosophy and the social science course on government, economics, and sociology. And the student of world affairs will be seriously handicapped if in his undergraduate program he cannot learn the essential historical facts which underlie so many of today's international problems.

One interesting approach to history, which seems at once to avoid the excesses historians fear and still has the advantages of general education, has been found by the State University of Iowa, Iowa State College, Ohio State University, and Clark University. These institutions keep the historical frame somewhat

[42] Charles C. Cole, Jr., "History in a General Education Program at Columbia College," *Journal of Higher Education*, XXVII (1956), 359–63.

[43] See Raymond P. Stearns, "College History and Its New Approaches," *School and Society*, LXXXII (Aug. 20, 1955), 49–55.

narrower in time, but broader in geography. Taking account of their students' work in secondary school in United States history, they each offer a course covering European and American history. The first half of this course (1500 to 1815) treats colonial America, but as part of the colonial expansion of Europe and the Europeanization of the world. In the second half the general movements and chronology from 1815 to 1848 are first discussed in terms of liberalism, reaction, and the revolutions of 1848; next, the course concentrates on nationalism between 1848 and 1870; and then it treats big labor and business as they developed from 1870 to 1914, comparing and contrasting the European and American scenes, as well as the international relations of the period. Then from 1918 to the present, the course proceeds decade by decade, evaluating the United States' impact on Europe and the growing role of the United States as a world power. The instructors assign source materials in politics and economics to illustrate the philosophies of the various periods and to enhance the student's understanding of history.[44]

In these courses, the associations made between the United States and European history remedy the usual defects of studying American history by itself, and the emphasis on the historical structure of Western civilization, with the United States placed in perspective, is very valuable to a student of world affairs. The supplemental readings can go far in keeping the courses from being lists of dates or kings or wars, but, on the other hand, the emphasis on history gives the students a perspective they may miss if the structure of history disappears in vapors arising from "the spirit of the age."

Most faculties are aware that it would be desirable for students to know more about the history of Russia and the Far East, and some instructors now emphasize more than they have in the past those contacts Russia and the Far Eastern countries have had with

[44] George L. Mosse, "Freshman History: Reality or Metaphysics?" *The Social Studies,* XLIX (1949), 99–103.

the West. But they cannot remedy the deficiency in full unless the colleges add courses about these areas to the required curriculum. One approach employed by Pennsylvania College for Women (now Chatham College) recently was to require students to take a World Culture course, which supplemented the college's course in Western Civilization by covering the history of Russian political developments since 1914, the internal political and economic reorganization since that time, and the patterns of tension-alliance-tension before, during, and after World War II. Events in China and Japan were reviewed from the Open Door Policy and the opening of Japan to the West, and students gave some attention as well to India. The course also had a Latin American unit, concentrating on Mexico, Brazil, and Argentina.[45] Chatham now offers a World Issues course which the college hopes will stimulate "global thinking" and help students understand the cultural and political influences on the relations among nations.

In another approach to the problem, the University of Kansas has developed a group of area survey courses which are interdisciplinary in nature and use faculty members from a wide number of departments to talk on the diverse elements of culture. Although the university does not require students to take these courses, they are open to all juniors and seniors as electives.[46] The University of California (Berkeley) makes available an all-Asia survey course, which in two semesters integrates the civilization and history of China, Japan, India, and Southeast Asia. The course is admittedly ambitious, but it very effectively introduces American students to Asia, and neatly supplements parallel offerings in the history of Western civilization.[47]

These efforts are steps in the right direction, for, without un-

[45] Mabel A. Elliott, "The Basic Curriculum in the Social Sciences at Pennsylvania College for Women," in McGrath, *Social Science*, pp. 136–37.

[46] See Hilden Gibson and Walter Sandelius, "General Education in the Social Sciences at the University of Kansas," in *ibid.*, pp. 151–52.

[47] Woodbridge Bingham, "An Integrated Approach in an All-Asia Survey Course," Association of American Colleges, *Bulletin*, XLIV (1958), 408–15.

derstanding what are no longer remote areas of the world, Americans are likely to continue being surprised by events there, as many were by the Korean War. To many people in the United States the events of 1950 seemed capricious and inexplicable; to students of Far Eastern history, however, who knew the part Korea has played in conflicts between Japan and China, the intervention of the Communist Chinese against a seeming threat from Korea had a historical continuity going back to the six-year war between China and Japan concerning Korea in 1590. We perhaps would conduct our foreign policy more wisely if we knew more history.[48] Colleges cannot themselves provide all the history students need, but it might be possible for more colleges and secondary schools to plan their curricula to make such good use of the time available for teaching history that Americans might acquire some more complete sense of the past.[49]

Taken together, the humanities and history have obviously a great deal to contribute to students' understanding of world affairs. In literature and language teaching, English and non-English, it is clear that faculties have done a great deal and can do much more to make students aware of other peoples and their ways of life. The individual instructor can often, by using his imagination, sharpen the student's understanding of world affairs. But he faces three barriers to further progress, which he can hurdle only with considerable outside help—the absence of adequate materials in non-Western languages, the failure of humanists and social scientists to work out together the most effective ways of including world affairs material in foreign language courses, and the inadequate language training in secondary schools.

---

[48] See Louis J. Halle, "History and the Present," *Virginia Quarterly Review*, XXXI (1955), 497–504.

[49] For other views on this subject, see C. B. A. Behrens, "History and the Universities," *Twentieth Century*, CLX (1956), 330–38; James High, "History in General Education," *Social Education*, XXI (1957), 56–58.

Historians, for their part, can illuminate their teaching and contribute effectively to students' understanding of world affairs by making their courses as international as history is itself. By indicating the ties between the subject matter of their courses and events that have occurred and are going on elsewhere in the world, they can make clear to students the great complexity of world affairs in various historical periods and point out the changing nature of international relations and diplomacy over whatever span of time their courses cover.[50]

Some institutions, as already noted, place history among the social sciences, which is the second of the three fields we must examine.

[50] See Stephen Duggan, "History, Politics, and Foreign Affairs," in Institute of International Education, *News Bulletin,* XX (Feb. 1, 1945), 4; and Arnold Toynbee, "The Writing of History," *Times Literary Supplement* (London), Aug. 15, 1958, p. xxv.

# CHAPTER FOUR

# Social Science and World Affairs

It seems clear to me that God designed us to live in society —just as He has given the bee the honey; and as our social system could not subsist without the sense of justice and injustice, He has given us the power to acquire that sense.

VOLTAIRE, in a letter to Frederick the Great

SOCIAL SCIENTISTS in American colleges and universities are primarily concerned with helping students understand the social order and the way men behave toward one another. Many of the problems these scholars are wrestling with today preoccupied Plato and Aristotle; some of them are as old as civilization itself. But the centuries have not yielded any unanimity about the best ways of approaching these difficult questions. Most recently, scholars have glimpsed the possibility of a scientific approach to social problems, and the desire to achieve genuine objectivity in analyzing human situations has thrown the social sciences into turmoil.

Instability in the social sciences exists also because social scientists have still to decide just what part of their learning they may appropriately teach in a liberal arts institution. This problem does not differ in kind from that which teachers of the humanities and natural sciences face. It is, however, quite different in degree, because insofar as the social scientists pretend to guide human beings in their communal behavior, their teaching is inevitably to some extent vocational.

More serious quandaries arise, though, from the ambiguous nature of social sciences. We have already seen that many historians assert frankly, and perhaps proudly, that history is both an art and a science. Many social scientists, by contrast, are trying as hard as they can to avoid or minimize any such duality in their own fields. The prevailing mood is to identify social science with the natural sciences rather than the humanities, and the search for objectivity has given rise to intensive and extensive experiments designed to adapt to the social sciences the methods of natural science and mathematics. No one has yet found, however, a way of escaping, especially in the more important questions, the immense role that values play in social issues.

Some social scientists try, in their teaching and research, to minimize the place of values and norms; others believe that unless social scientists give primary attention to problems of value, they are ignoring the humane essence of their work and are dooming themselves to deal only with unimportant trivialities susceptible of measurement. All would agree, however, that the problem of finding the proper place in the social sciences for facts and for values has divided scholars into a number of camps, many of whose warriors neither can nor wish to speak the language of their opponents.[1]

Such differences naturally limit the amount of cooperation possible among social scientists. They also affect the study of world affairs and explain in part why educational institutions differ so in defining social science and in the number of courses they require undergraduates to take in this general field.

Some institutions, for example, classify history as a social science, and it alone may suffice to meet a social science requirement,

[1] See report by Horace Taylor and David McCord Wright quoted in Henry W. Ehrmann, "American Higher Education and the Social Sciences," *The Teaching of the Social Sciences in the United States* (Paris: Unesco, 1954), pp. 29–33; Leonard D. White (ed.), *The State of the Social Sciences* (Chicago: University of Chicago Press, 1956); Roland Young (ed.), *Approaches to the Study of Politics* (Evanston, Ill.: Northwestern University Press, 1958); and Dwight Waldo, *Political Science in the United States of America* (Paris: Unesco, 1956).

as, for instance, at the University of Virginia. Where history comprises the entire social science requirement, emphasizing world affairs in history courses becomes especially important. Some colleges which regard history as a social science offer students a choice of other social sciences by which they may fulfill their requirements, as at Bowdoin College, where students must undertake four semesters' work in at least two of the social sciences, defined for this purpose as economics, government, history, sociology, and philosophy.

Because the social sciences have developed along so many different, specialized lines, faculties have to decide how much of each subject to require students to study. They have filled the social science portion of the undergraduate fare with various combinations of courses. However, two basic patterns predominate. The traditional (and still most common) college program allows students to choose one or more introductory courses from among the social sciences. Other institutions use an interdisciplinary approach, of which the second year of Contemporary Civilization at Columbia College is probably the oldest and best-established example. In contrast with the traditional approach, this course does not introduce the student to some or all of the social sciences in turn. Instead, the course exposes students to ideas important in Western society, and the faculty considers it less important for a student to identify the ideas as "sociology," "psychology," or "government" than for him to grasp the broader issues with which the various social sciences deal.

Some colleges offer both types of courses and allow students to select the approach they themselves prefer. At the University of Oregon, for instance, all candidates for the bachelor of arts degree must include in their programs two course sequences in the social sciences. To satisfy the requirement, they may choose offerings in individual subjects (in this case, anthropology, economics, geography, history, philosophy, political science, psychology, religion, or sociology) or courses in General Social

Science. Included in the category General Social Science are courses on Social Science and Social Policy, an integrated introduction to social science; a history course, covering significant events, ideas, and institutions in the development of Western civilization; and The Study of Society, a survey of the subject matter and methods of the social sciences.

## Interdisciplinary Courses

The interdisciplinary courses in the social sciences have explored world affairs in a number of interesting ways. At the University of Wisconsin, for instance, there is a social science course in the Program of Integrated Liberal Studies which devotes the last of four semesters to The International Scene. In the preceding three units, the students take up Early Man and His Society, The Transition to Industrial Society, and Modern Industrial Society—The United States. Simultaneously, the students study in their humanities course the literary and artistic contributions of the ancient, medieval, Renaissance, and modern American societies. In the final portion of their humanities course, while they study American literature, art, philosophy, and architecture after 1850, they take up in their social science course such topics as the geographic, economic, social, and political factors tending to create a world society; the conflicts within that society; and the methods, ranging from war to world government, by which men have attempted to resolve their conflicts. The students examine the elements of national power in the major states, in selected minor states, and also in the more critical problem areas of the world not yet organized as states. The semester provides an excellent capstone to a course which applies the analytical tools of the social sciences to domestic society and depicts the way today's social institutions have evolved from ancient Greece through the ages.[2]

[2] Richard Hartshorne and Robert C. Pooley, "The Social Studies in Wisconsin's Program of Integrated Studies," in Earl J. McGrath, *Social Science in*

Taking up international problems in one semester, as this course does, is by no means the only possible way of dealing with international affairs in a social science course. At the University of Chicago, material on international problems appears throughout the syllabi of three sequential social science courses. As the students explore the several social science disciplines, they examine the way the disciplines can throw light on world affairs. The Chicago courses are designed to help students understand how American institutions, ideals, and problems have developed; how to apply the scientific method to the quest for knowledge of human nature and society; and how, as citizens, to deliberate rationally about problems of public policy. The courses draw in varying degrees and combinations on the social sciences, and in each course the students give some attention to international problems. For example, in the first quarter of Social Sciences 1, after examining the origins of American democracy, the building of the American nation, and American democracy in the Agrarian Age (1789–1861), the students devote a week to the way the United States developed a foreign policy between 1793 and 1823, and study the beginnings of isolation, neutrality, and the Monroe Doctrine.

In the second quarter the students take up such topics as American Democracy in the Industrial Age and ways of interpreting history, but in the third quarter they study American Imperialism in the Industrial Age, taking up sea power and the moral aspect of war, the debate in the United States over imperialism, problems that imperialism poses for a democracy, and imperialism in Latin America. The classes in Social Science 1 study the story of World War I, America's entry into the war, and the origins of the League of Nations. Then, after looking at domestic affairs from 1919 on, students examine the United States' part in World War II and subsequent events and trace the evolution of mod-

---

*General Education* (Dubuque, Iowa: William C. Brown Co., 1949), pp. 199–209.

ern American foreign policy, the origins and role of the United Nations, the clash with the Soviet Union, and problems of international organization.

Social Sciences 2 at Chicago concentrates on personality and culture, the interaction between them, and the effect on the individual of the modern industrial system. The course draws heavily on psychology and sociology, but also includes some economics and philosophy. The students try to determine the nature of culture, the industrial system, war, and national loyalties; they try to see whether there is a common human nature and whether it is possible to control war and create a world community.

In Social Sciences 3, the students take up questions of public policy, such as self-determination; theory and practice of international politics, domestic and international economic policies, world trade; the theoretical bases of socialism, communism, and fascism; and the nature of international consensus.[3]

Courses using the case method, a technique employed by Stephens College, have obvious opportunities to include international problems. One section of the Stephens social science course looks at America in the Family of Nations and considers the causes of World War II, conflicts in the postwar world, basic factors in American foreign policy, and the problem of world organization. These issues follow a study of the principal philosophical, economic, social, and political problems of the United States.[4]

## Sociology and Anthropology

Sociologists and anthropologists, in their own courses, can contribute in distinctive ways to a student's understanding of world affairs. First of all, in setting forth the nature of their fields, they

[3] Milton B. Singer, "The Social Sciences Program in the College of the University of Chicago," in McGrath, *Social Science*, pp. 37–74.

[4] John A. Decker, "The Contemporary Social Issues Course at Stephens College," in *ibid.*, pp. 210–26.

can stress the international nature of their methodology, their debts not only to ancient observers of society like Plato, Aristotle, and the legendary Manu, or the fourteenth-century historian-philosopher Ibn Khaldun, but also to a distinguished roster of Western Europeans and Americans.

An introductory course in sociology, which conventionally discusses the way social groups originate, maintain themselves, and disintegrate, cannot but broaden a student's understanding of world affairs in many ways. According to one regional survey, instructors of introductory sociology courses want most of all to help students understand the society in which they live.[5] Course descriptions, and sometimes even the titles themselves, as at the University of Minnesota, where the first semester of a three-semester introductory course is called Man in Modern Society, often reflect this intention. Certainly a conscientious attempt to fulfill this objective requires sociologists to pay considerable attention to the role of the nation-state and cultural contacts in world affairs.

It is entirely appropriate, for instance, for students of sociology to set the concrete problems of world affairs in the broad context of relations among all human groups from the family to the entire human race. They may put the nation-state and international organizations in perspective by attempting to determine how permanent the national and international institutions are, how their functions and social structure relate to each other, how unified in purpose the members are, and how natural or artificial the groups are. They may also investigate the number and kinds of activities which states and international organizations engage in, how complex they are, and how citizens do or do not participate in managing their affairs. Such analyses can be extremely useful correctives for the political and legal approaches to world

---

[5] A. L. Ferriss, " 'Introductory Sociology' in the South-eastern States: 1950," *Social Forces*, XXIX (1951), 298.

problems which usually assume the very social structure the sociologists attempt to analyze.[6]

It is, of course, especially gratifying to find advanced sociology courses dealing with these problems specifically, as for instance, at Ohio State, which offers Social Organization in a Changing World. This course takes up the adaptability of contemporary institutions to new social pressures and the impact of United States problems on world culture. Another course of interest is World Community, offered by Boston University, which the Sociology Department recommends especially to majors in the combined field of philosophy and sociology, and which takes up the social and psychological aspects of world organization and the way the world organizations relate to such values as peace and justice.

In addition to illuminating the nature of the state and international organization, sociologists, especially in their advanced courses, can help students become aware of demographic problems and their implications for society. Most sociology departments offer courses in population under various titles, for example, Introduction to Population Problems (Princeton), Introduction to the Study of Population and Human Ecology (Chicago), Population (Miami University, North Carolina, Tulane), Population Problems (Michigan), World Migration (Western Reserve), World Population and Social Structure (Oregon), and World Population Problems (Minnesota).

Both sociologists and anthropologists have important contributions to make in offering courses about the social systems of nation-states and the cultural patterns of diverse parts of the world, although only the largest institutions can afford to offer separate courses on every major region. Comparing several diverse cultural groups in one course, however, is a method which

---

[6] See Wright, *The Study of International Relations* (New York: Appleton-Century-Crofts, 1955), pp. 395–98, and Robert C. Angell, "Sociology and the World Crisis," *American Sociological Review*, XVI (1951), 749–57.

has advantages for both colleges and students and is widely practiced, for example, in Anthropological Studies of Contemporary Nations (Harvard), Contemporary Civilization (Colorado), Cultural Areas of the World (Michigan State), Cultural Worlds (Colorado), Culture History (Hobart and William Smith Colleges), Natural Cultures and World Society (Michigan), and Peoples of the World (Miami). At Colgate and the University of Wisconsin, moreover, the Anthropology Department offers courses in cultural contact and acculturation, and at California (Berkeley), Michigan, and Harvard the anthropologists offer a wide variety of courses in the cultural history of regions, which are especially valuable for students studying particular areas of the world. A number of anthropology departments, furthermore, offer undergraduate courses in language and culture (for example, California [Berkeley], Indiana, and Yale), which contain many useful insights for students of the humanities as well as those of the social sciences.

Such courses should help students to understand diverse cultural patterns; to see their own culture in perspective; to appreciate the impact of culture on world affairs; and to observe the habits, ideas, and attitudes which groups share and transmit to future generations as a social heritage. This cultural interpenetration is among the commonest of historical phenomena, and the story of cultural borrowings demonstrates a degree of human interdependence of which too few students are aware. Advanced courses on social disorganization and on contacts among cultural and racial groups are especially important in this regard and are available to upperclassmen at many colleges and universities, including Bates, Brown, Colorado, Hawaii, Michigan, Missouri, Princeton, St. Lawrence (New York), Wisconsin, and Yale.

The significance of cultural contacts is by no means only historical. Modern transportation and communications make an increasing number of intercultural contacts inevitable, not only among civil servants, but among private citizens, and representatives of nongovernmental organizations as well. Cultural activities have become in many cases instruments of national policy, and states are becoming more and more conscious of the need to have stimulating cultural exchange programs. Moreover, international economic development programs, bilateral and multilateral, can only succeed to the extent that those engaged in them can make successful cultural contacts. It is therefore most important for students, many of whom will themselves later make these contacts as tourists, artists, propagandists, technical experts, or administrators, to have some idea of why and how certain social systems clash and the conditions under which one group may successfully transmit its culture to another. Without that understanding there is no way to avoid the disastrous effects of uninformed and unthinking cross-cultural encounters.

More than any other people today, Americans need to know how to analyze their own culture for its strengths and weaknesses; to appreciate what other cultures have to offer in terms of their customs, arts and crafts, humanistic studies, science, and technology; and to contribute acceptably to the ways of life of others.[7] It is particularly gratifying, therefore, to find courses in comparative social institutions giving specific attention to the problems of cultural contact and technological change (Ohio State), to the difficulties of modernizing underdeveloped areas (Princeton), and to the impact of Western civilization upon nonliterate peoples (Yale).

Unfortunately, clashes among cultures have not been sufficiently well understood, and the United States has already suffered from arrogance on the part of some of the more than one million Americans serving abroad as civilians or in the Armed Forces. Guy Mollet has denounced as "semi-Marxism" the "half-baked notions" (in Catlin's phrase) held by some American per-

[7] See "National Programs of International Cultural Relations," *International Conciliation*, No. 642 (June 1950), pp. 301–36, and Alex Inkeles, "Understanding a Foreign Society: A Sociologist's View," *World Politics*, III (1951), 269–80.

sonnel administering American aid programs overseas who believed that

industrialization over-night is "a good thing"; . . . that mere production is a good thing whatever the cultural consequences, e.g., in a rural, Buddhist country such as Burma; and [flaunted] . . . their Occidental patronizing attitude and their latent notion that gratitude should be automatic, mechanically following from dollar bounties.[8]

## Psychology

Psychology offers many important insights to students of world affairs, as well as to students of all the social sciences, even though, more than any other social science, it relates to the natural sciences, especially the biological sciences. It treats of living things, and in its attempts to understand man's mind and explain his behavior, it draws on anatomy and physiology. Where it studies vision, hearing, and touch, it relates to physics; and in analyzing taste and smell, to chemistry. General psychology courses, therefore, conventionally include biological, physical, and chemical aspects of human behavior. The focus on the entire man and on the behavior of men distinguishes the principal concern of psychology from that of the other sciences, however, especially where it studies emotions, instincts, intelligence, and consciousness.

Colleges often, with considerable justice, classify psychology as a social science. General psychology courses can properly serve as alternatives to the other social sciences, however, only if they actually do touch on social behavior. When the course does not include some social psychology, it more properly belongs among the natural sciences, which is, for example, where Harvard places its introductory psychology course, and even a general education course in Human Behavior. Fortunately for students seeking psychological insights into world affairs, social psychology does in fact receive more attention now than in the past in most gen-

8 M. Guy Mollet, speech in April 1956, quoted by George Catlin, *On Political Goals* (New York: St. Martin's Press, 1957), pp. 46–47.

eral psychology courses, texts, laboratory manuals, and collateral readings.

Admittedly students cannot consider social psychology in detail in general psychology courses, for it is in itself a highly specialized study. But it has proved possible even in basic psychology courses to take up individual psychological processes, such as learning and perception, in a social context, and to teach about the ways in which groups influence individual attitudes and beliefs. With an eye on the social aspects of their subject, psychologists obviously can help students to understand themselves in a world setting. They can assist them to analyze their role as members of the nation and of private associations with international connections, like the National Council of the Churches of Christ or the International Chamber of Commerce, and as citizens of nation-states which are members of international public organizations like Unesco. The nature of man's loyalty to the state and his relations to international organizations and their officials, to foreigners, and to educational and informational media also have a place in the required psychology course. Such a course should help a student appreciate the way his own psychological characteristics compare with universal aspects of human nature and help him understand how man's inheritance relates to his experience, his personality to his culture, and his unconscious drives to his conscious intentions.

When students can go on to take the one course or sometimes, as at Boston, Kenyon, and Williams, two courses in social psychology often available as an elective in either the sociology or psychology department,[9] their instructors have excellent opportunities to take up the psychological aspects of nationalism, the role of public opinion in world affairs, international implications of racial relations, intercultural contacts, and propaganda. Such matters arise naturally in courses in social psychology, which cus-

[9] William Bruce Cameron, Philip Lasley, and Richard Dewey, "Who Teaches Social Psychology?" *American Sociological Review*, XV (1950), 553-55.

tomarily deal, among other topics, with motivation, learning, prejudice, culture and personality, social or group norms, prestige, perception and communication, media of mass communication, leadership, and collective behavior.

Social psychology, very often under that title, appears frequently in the sociology and psychology departments of the nation's colleges. These departments also offer other courses on aspects of social psychology which relate to world affairs. One of the most frequent is Collective Behavior, which is available at Akron, Brown, Carleton, Dartmouth, Hawaii, Hood, Kentucky, Ohio State, Missouri, South Dakota, Wisconsin, among others. Some colleges offer additional courses in communications and opinion (North Carolina), cultural patterns and the individual (Colgate and Ohio State), individual and race differences (Saint Louis University), mass communications and modern society (Hobart and William Smith Colleges, Tufts, Yale), personality and culture (Alabama, Indiana, California [Berkeley]), personality and social behavior (Chicago and Yale), psychology of social movements (Allegheny and Michigan State), social factors in personality (Illinois), social pathology (Antioch, Hood, and Western Reserve), and sociological study of communications (Chicago, Columbia, Yale).[10]

√ These courses in social psychology, like the related courses in sociology, bear on national programs of intercultural exchange, but they are also very important because of the growing significance of national and international informational programs conducted by governmental groups like the Voice of America, private groups like Radio Free Europe, and international agencies like the United Nations. How important these broadcasts can be and how relevant they are in world affairs has become increasingly clear in recent years. In Hungary in 1956, for instance, a number of revolutionists seem to have been tragically misled by the con-

10 See Wilbert S. Ray, "The Teaching of Social Psychology," in Ehrmann, *The Teaching of the Social Sciences . . .* , pp. 124–28.

tent of some Western-sponsored broadcasts which erroneously implied that United States or United Nations aid was imminent. And more recently, in the Middle East, some observers have suggested that broadcasts by Arab radio stations have been responsible for aggravating much of the unrest in the area.

The psychology of international relations is an extremely elusive subject. Students who have taken psychology courses conducted with an eye on world affairs should, however, be able at least to appreciate the complex relations lying behind the statement in the preamble to the Unesco Constitution that wars begin in the minds of men. They should also have some better idea of the character of states and world politics as they examine the attitudes, interests, mechanisms, and tensions of individual minds and the conditions of culture and public opinion in which particular institutions function. In an era when public opinion, education, communications, technology, and methods of warfare and aggression are changing, it is urgent for students to know how specialists are attempting to apply the insights of sociology and psychology to world affairs.[11]

## Political Science

The most common beginning course in political science is the course in American government. Traditionally it emphasizes political institutions and functions, and it can do a great deal to help students understand world affairs if it includes a study of the ways the United States develops its foreign policy and the machinery for conducting world affairs. In describing the various branches of the government, instructors can easily point out the constitutional provisions relating to foreign affairs, the role of the President in formulating and carrying out foreign policy, the effect Congress has upon our foreign affairs by exercising its power to tax and supervise finances and administration, the special responsibilities of the Senate in regard to treaties and ambassadors,

[11] See Wright, *The Study of International Relations,* pp. 416–17, 424–25.

the conflict between local and national interests, particularly in the House of Representatives, and the role of the Supreme Court in establishing and interpreting principles of international law.

Introductory courses in political science are undoubtedly affected by the contemporary emphasis in the field on the behavioral approach to political phenomena. Primarily concerned about the behavior patterns which reflect power and influence in the process of governing, the political behaviorists are attempting to discover uniform patterns in the ways men actually behave. They rely as much as possible on empirical methods and try to make their research and teaching rigorously systematic. Behavioral materials have for a long time been important to students of political campaigns, voting, elections, politics, parties, pressure groups, and public opinion. There is, moreover, a growing body of literature which now combines public opinion study techniques and an interest in problems of international relations.[12] Instructors in beginning courses may draw from these studies illustrations from the international field, which show the connections between domestic and international politics and the ways that political scientists deal with both.

It is also possible in introductory courses in political science, which must inevitably touch on the proper place in political studies of fact and of value, to illustrate the problem of ascertaining the proper role of both with material drawn from the international field. The debate between the "realists" who have argued that the traditional study of international relations has been handicapped by "utopianism," "sentimentalism," "moral-

[12] See, for example, Ralph H. Smuckler, "The Region of Isolationism," *American Political Science Review*, XLVII (1953), 386–401; Gabriel A. Almond, *The American People and Foreign Policy* (New York: Harcourt, Brace & Co., 1950), and G. A. Almond, *et al.*, *The Appeals of Communism* (Princeton, N. J.: Princeton University Press, 1954); Otto Klineberg, *Tensions Affecting International Understanding* (New York: Social Science Research Council, 1950); Hadley Cantril, *How Nations See Each Other: A Study in Public Opinion* (Urbana: University of Illinois Press, 1953); Frederick S. Dunn, *War and the Minds of Men* (New York: Harper & Bros., 1950). For references to other works, see Waldo, p. 59.

ism," and "legalism," and those who have argued that idealism is part of ultimate reality has produced so voluminous a literature in the past few years that there is a wealth of material available to political scientists.[13] For the student concerned with international relations, the problem facing all social scientists of how or whether to exclude values from the "scientific" study of social problems is acute.

All introductory courses in political science are to some extent theoretical, and there is room in them, as in the introductions to the other social sciences, to stress the international roster of theorists who have contributed to man's ideas on politics. In all introductory courses in political science, theoretical or otherwise, instructors should try where possible to relate the ideas of political thinkers outside the United States to American political thought, to show the impact of French and English ideas on the American Revolution, and contrast our government with those of other major powers in the world with different parliamentary systems, such as England and France, and with the Soviet Union, as the leading example of Communist dictatorship. Such comparisons are possible, although, of course, in different degrees, in elementary courses in American government, political theory, or comparative government, as well as in advanced courses in these same subjects.

Two interesting variations on the introductory course are offered by Rutgers and Brown Universities. Rutgers permits non-majors to substitute for American Government a course in Basic Political Issues, which takes up not only domestic problems, but problems on the international scene as well. And Brown offers as an alternative to its introductory course in Principles of Political Science a course in the Idea of World Peace, which takes up the theoretical proposals for world organization from the time of the Abbé de St. Pierre to the present.

[13] For an excellent introduction to the problem and the existing literature, see Waldo, pp. 60–61.

## Economics

Economists can contribute distinctively to the study of world affairs in teaching students about the way man supplies his material needs and wants. They can present, among other things, the theoretical work of a distinguished roster of men from many countries, the importance of economics in world history, the impact of such doctrines as mercantilism and *laissez faire,* and the place of economics in today's ideological conflicts.

Showing how economics relates to contemporary problems is obviously important for the nonspecialist, but it has so far been very difficult to prepare beginning courses along these lines. Economists have a highly developed body of theoretical ideas, which conventionally make up the beginning course, although some instructors focus students' attention on economic institutions and teach only so much theory as they need for this purpose.[14] In this regard, the economists seem to differ from other social scientists, who have found it possible to relate theory and practice for beginning students and reserve detailed theoretical studies for future specialists. It should be possible, however, to introduce students effectively to economics and at the same time expose them to the practical economic facts and problems of their time. A course illustrating economic theory with contemporary case studies could help students appreciate the importance of economic motives in imperialism and war and the conflicts between political and economic motives in formulating state policy. In such a course the student would also study the clashes between capitalism and communism and between economic nationalists and internationalists. Even in presenting theory, economists might well show their students how important maximum production and equitable distribution are for the well-being of the world; how rational economic policies are some-

14 Horace Taylor, "The Teaching of Economics in the United States," *The University Teaching of Social Sciences: Economics* ([Paris]: Unesco, 1954), pp. 243–44, and "The Teaching of Undergraduate Economics," *American Economic Review,* XL (December 1950), Part 2, especially 2–8, 57–58.

times frustrated by international politics; and how world resources, population trends, and technological developments affect international politics.[15] The general student should also know something about the problems of underdeveloped countries and about international economic cooperation through the specialized agencies and the Economic and Social Council of the United Nations. Instructors can even arrange for students to use United Nations economic publications in their courses.

International economics is admittedly a highly specialized subject, but beginning students should be able to learn something about it. Economists are paying more and more attention to international economic problems,[16] but it would be regrettable to limit attention to such problems to the graduate level.

Taken separately or as a group, the social sciences hold innumerable attractions for students concerned with world affairs. No other courses can teach them more directly about the complexity of human societies, the nature of "community," and the behavior of human beings. The interdisciplinary social science courses may contain whole units of work on some aspect of world affairs or examine specific problems of world affairs; sociology and anthropology can open the students' eyes to the structure of groups and the difficulties of organizing a world society; psychology and social psychology can help the students analyze man's behavior, rational and irrational, alone and in groups; political science can focus their attention on power; and economics can call to their notice international trade and the impact of domestic economic forces on world affairs. Students of all these disciplines, moreover, owe a considerable debt to an international roster of theorists, whose work alone, in proper perspective, can do much to show students the interdependence of men in advancing the frontiers of the mind.

[15] See Wright, *The Study of International Relations*, pp. 263–64.
[16] Taylor, p. 258.

# CHAPTER FIVE

# *Natural Science, Mathematics, and World Affairs*

> For out of olde feldes, as men seyth,
> Cometh al this newe corn fro yer to yere;
> And out of olde bookes, in good feyth,
> Cometh al this newe science that men lere.
>
> GEOFFREY CHAUCER, *Parliament of Fowles*

As WE HAVE SEEN, studying the humanities and social sciences is wholly consonant with studying world affairs. But of all the fields of learning, few are so without national boundaries as the natural sciences and mathematics and few have greater implications now for world affairs. For colleges and universities not to make these facts clear to all their students, majors in science and nonmajors, could prove dangerous for everyone. The future scientist must understand how international politics have made it inevitable that government will play a growing role in his life, and he must appreciate the concomitant public responsibilities which devolve upon him. The nonmajor, on the other hand, must comprehend the international ramifications of science and the ways in which science affects the world he lives in if he is to support the scientist in his demands for the freedom and facilities needed to pursue basic research.

Both majors in science and nonmajors should become aware in their educational pursuits of the ways in which science has often transformed politics and how governments have always been concerned with science, at least to the point of applying inventions to public purposes. Warfare and international relations have been completely altered by discoveries like gunpowder and the airplane and by the technological revolutions precipitated when science harnessed steam and split the atom.[1] But as technology has become more complex and expensive and as national and international well-being have come to depend increasingly on science, governments are playing a far larger part in the lives of scientists and the future of science.

The expanding interest of government in science is perfectly evident in the United States. The association between the two goes back to the founding of the Republic, for the Constitution in Article 1, Section 8, grants to Congress the power to issue patents, and the Botanic Garden, which collects, cultivates, and distributes the vegetable products of this and other countries for the benefit of medicine, nutrition, manufacture, and the arts, traces its origins back to 1818. Abraham Lincoln signed a bill in 1863 establishing the National Academy of Sciences to report to the government "upon any subject of science or art"; and Woodrow Wilson created the National Research Council in 1916 as a measure of national preparedness.

When Franklin Roosevelt established the Office of Scientific Research and Development, which operated from 1941–45, scientists became full and responsible partners with government.

Today, the government is more involved with science than ever before: the Atomic Energy Commission, created in 1946, directs the development, control, and use of atomic energy; the National Science Foundation, established in 1950, tries to develop and encourage a national policy to initiate, promote, support, and evaluate basic research and education in the sciences;

[1] See, for instance, William Fielding Ogburn (ed.), *Technology and International Relations* (Chicago: University of Chicago Press, 1949); Linden Mander, *Foundations of Modern International Society* (rev. ed.; Stanford: Stanford University Press, 1947).

and the President's Science Advisory Committee, established in 1951 and transferred to the White House in 1957, advises the Chief Executive in matters relating to science and technology. The President also has a Special Assistant for Science and Technology and a National Committee for the Development of Scientists and Engineers (established in 1956) to stimulate nongovernmental efforts to improve training and increase the numbers of scientists and engineers. The Department of Defense, of course, is vitally concerned with research, engineering, atomic energy, and guided missiles. In 1958, the Pentagon established the Advanced Research Projects Agency and gave it special responsibility for military projects for outer space. The civilian agency directing the peaceful exploration of outer space, also established in 1958, is the National Aeronautics and Space Administration.

Government concern for science does not stop here, however. The National Bureau of Standards, created in 1901, conducts scientific and technical programs in a wide range of fields: applied mathematics, atomic and radiation physics, basic instrumentation, building technology, chemistry, cryogenic engineering, data processing systems, electricity and electronics, heat, mechanics, metallurgy, mineral products, optics and metrology, organic and fibrous materials, radio propagation physics and engineering, radio standards, and weights and measures. The Department of Agriculture has for years gone to the far corners of the earth to find new and better varieties of produce and livestock, as the names of a large number of plants and animals (Red Egyptian wheat, Manchurian barley, Guernsey cows, and Danish hogs) illustrate. Moreover, the Agricultural Research Service carries on physical, biological, chemical, and engineering research on behalf of farmers and farming. And in 1951 the Department of State added a science adviser to its staff and began to work with the National Science Foundation through scientific attachés in our embassies to keep this country posted on international scientific developments and to facilitate the work of

American scientists abroad. The government allowed this program to lapse in 1953, but planned to renew it in 1959. Among the other government agencies working closely with scientists are the Public Health Service, the Federal Aviation Agency, the Bureau of Mines, the Geological Survey, and the Weather Bureau.[2] Scientific progress is now so closely intertwined with government, the nation's laboratories and government so inextricably connected, that most scientists will find themselves at some point in their careers working in or for the government, in laboratories, public or private, on matters of defense; as advisers to the President and government agencies; or as experts abroad on technical assistance missions.

The implications for science of the growing number of ties with government are profound. Problems of politics and administration, once quite foreign to the research-minded investigator in his laboratory, become matters of enormous consequence for the success or failure of his work. How to keep sufficient numbers of scientists working at basic research when the incentives to carry on applied research for government and industry are so great becomes a major problem. Questions of public policy become inextricably bound up with scientific progress: How much public money should be spent on science? How should the government supervise these public funds and evaluate the research? Who should administer government-financed research—the military, the civilian departments, international organizations, universities, or industry? What role should the military services play in scientific research? What security measures are essential for national safety, and what measures impede scientific research?

[2] *United States Government Organization Manual, 1958-59* (Washington: Government Printing Office, 1958), *passim.* See also E. C. Stakman, "Science and International Understanding," *School Science and Mathematics,* LII (June 1952), 11–18; "Scientists To Go Abroad for U.S.," *New York Times,* Nov. 9, 1957, p. 10, and "U.S. Program To Post Scientists Abroad Lags," *ibid.,* May 9, 1958, p. 6; Vannevar Bush, *Modern Arms and Free Men* (New York: Simon & Schuster, 1949), p. 6; and Don K. Price, *Government in Science* (New York: New York University Press, 1954).

The difficulties of answering these questions are enormous. The basic issue, of course, is whether a democracy can mobilize the forces of science in its defense without impairing the progress of science or sacrificing the very values science is mobilized to defend? Recent history is not encouraging on this score, for it provides ample evidence that scientists have not been comfortable in their contacts with politics; that government security programs have severely damaged not only the reputations of many scientists but also the scientific programs financed by the government itself; that legislators, administrators, and the general public have not understood the nature of science; and that their failure to understand it has denied to the scientists the public support they have needed in their times of troubles.[3]

Not only must scientists understand the social effects of science; but also they must realize that their public responsibilities are greater today than ever before. Without understanding the nexus between science and society and without some sense of the social frame around their work, their lives may be frustrated and democratic society endangered.[4]

The nonscientist, in turn, must learn to appreciate the nature of science itself, including its intrinsic international character. To most scientists and mathematicians, the international aspect of their work is so obvious, they tend to take it for granted. It has by no means been so obvious to the nonscientists, however, and their failure to understand why scientists traditionally exchange information with one another across national frontiers resulted after World War II in supersecurity regulations in the

[3] The pages of the *Bulletin of the Atomic Scientists* provide the most accessible and formidable documentation of the difficulties scientists have encountered. See, for instance, Clifford Grobstein, "Federal Research and Development: Prospects 1954," IX (1953), 299–304; Lloyd V. Berkner, "Science and National Strength," IX (1953), 154–55 ff.; Nat S. Finney, "The Threat to Atomic Science," X (1954), 285–86 ff.; and Edward A. Shils, "Scientists, Administrators, and Politicians: The Report of the Riehlman Committee," X (1954), 371–74.

[4] See Lewis Mumford, "The Transformations of Man," in Andrew A. Freeman (ed.), *Brainpower Quest* (New York: Macmillan Co., 1957), pp. 82–83.

United States which lulled the country into a false sense of safety and adversely affected scientific progress in the Western world. Not knowing (or forgetting) that scientific research proceeds so uniformly that discoveries of the same phenomena have often occurred throughout history in widely separated areas of the world, and naïvely confident of the superiority of American know-how, many Americans mistakenly believed after 1945 that the United States could retain the secret of the atom bomb and were also tremendously shocked in 1957 when the Russians launched their sputnik. Too many had forgotten that scientific progress, even before 1957, did not owe everything to the United States. They rarely recalled that Russia had pioneers like Metchnikoff in biology or that a Frenchman, Pasteur, revolutionized medical practice. Many are not even now aware that a German, Robert Koch, discovered the tuberculosis germ; that one of his countrymen, Emil von Behring, made the first antitoxin serum for diphtheria; that radium was discovered by the Curies, a Frenchman and his wife of Polish extraction; and that a Canadian, F. G. Banting, isolated insulin for treating diabetes. Nor do they think much about (let alone remember the national origins of) men like Euclid, Ptolemy, Galileo, Descartes, and Newton. And the American feat of exploding the atom bomb has obscured for many Americans the debt that even modern atomic research owes to nationals of other countries: to Fermi (Italian), Szilard (Polish), Bohr (Danish), and to Einstein (German).

Atomic research only illustrates once again the universality of scientific genius. In the future, as in the past, scientists will need to cooperate across national frontiers; hence their enthusiasm for such spectacular cooperative efforts as the International Geophysical Year of 1957–58, the U.N. International Conferences on the Peaceful Uses of Atomic Energy in 1955 and 1958, and the potential efforts of the International Atomic Energy Agency. The success of much of the world's work depends largely on conditions of international peace and amity which allow research for peaceful purposes and encourage free exchanges of information among scientists; international scientific cooperation is, of course, by no means limited to the atomic field. Individual scientists and government agencies in this country and throughout the world continually maintain these contacts by working together through international organizations with important responsibilities in the fields of health, agriculture, communications, meteorology, and education. The World Health Organization, for instance, attempts to contain the spread of disease and keep public health authorities everywhere informed about epidemics. The Food and Agriculture Organization works to improve the world's diet, farming methods, and farm products; the United Nations Educational, Scientific, and Cultural Organization, to promote collaboration among the nations through education, science, and culture in order to further justice, the rule of law, and human rights and freedoms and to encourage the international exchange of information and personnel; the International Telecommunication Union, to establish economical systems of telecommunications throughout the world by regulating the international use of telegraph, telephone, and radio and, through services and scientific studies, to improve the means of communication; the International Civil Aviation Organization, to develop principles and techniques of international air navigation and to plan and develop international air transport; and the World Meteorological Organization to improve and coordinate meteorological observations and to encourage research and training in meteorology.

Despite these all-embracing international consequences of scientific work, courses in the natural sciences and mathematics pay very little attention to them. Even more than in the humanities or the social sciences, elementary instruction in mathematics, physics, chemistry, geology, zoology, botany, and biology has been designed primarily for those intending to take advanced work and concentrates on the detailed subject matter students need for further study. Instructors often plan such courses for students already strongly motivated to take them, and since each course treats only one subject, students often learn a great deal about one science, but little of any other, and still less about the importance of science in the world. The general student in science, as well as the future specialist, traditionally finds himself in courses which develop his technical vocabulary and laboratory skills, while systematically presenting him with the accumulated facts and theories of one particular science, but which pay little attention to his grasp of basic concepts of science and mathematics, their development, the great body of scientific literature, and the relation of the sciences to other areas of interest and activity. As the Harvard Committee put it, such courses frequently supply only the bricks of science. Students going on into more advanced work can build something from them, but the "general student is more likely to be left simply with bricks."[5]

Shocked by the narrow and specialized knowledge which many traditional courses gave nonspecialists, several faculties set about organizing natural science survey courses in the years immediately after World War I. These courses, popular in the late twenties and thirties, included material from all the sciences and mathematics and attempted to cover hurriedly as much as the separate courses which they replaced. These early efforts to remodel courses in science for nonscience students were, however, not successful, and faculties either changed them considerably or abandoned them entirely after a few years. Instructors and students inevitably adjudged the courses superficial miscellanies of little value to anyone.

Since World War II, faculties have taken another tack for the benefit of the nonmajor, and, instead of attempting to acquaint undergraduates with the ever-growing body of scientific fact, they have attempted to teach generally applicable laws and principles of science. Students must still acquire certain scientific facts, but

[5] *General Education in a Free Society* (Cambridge, Mass.: Harvard University Press, 1945), especially pp. 220–21.

not all the facts of any one science and certainly not all scientific facts, but only those facts necessary to illustrate the nature of science and to master the cases that may be used in the course. College teaching in the natural sciences goes forward today in two groups of courses: in the traditional elementary courses in the several sciences and in the courses inspired by the general education movement.[6] In either instance, colleges require students to study some science for their bachelor's degree either for one year or two, and most of them ask students to divide their work between the physical and biological sciences.[7]

Despite the variety of scientific courses now being offered in colleges using the general education approach, the typical course is a two-semester, six-credit, nonlaboratory course given by the lecture method with demonstrations and visual aids.[8] None of the newer courses attempts to cover a large body of material in all the sciences, as did the interwar courses, nor do they encompass all the details of one. They usually treat a few selected topics, laws, or problems in several sciences[9] in order to show students something of the methods of science, give them some facility in using scientific techniques, and acquaint them with leading scientific principles, laws, and concepts. Many instructors are nonetheless also trying to demonstrate to students the impact of

[6] In figures made available in 1950, 5 percent of 720 colleges replying to a questionnaire offered general education courses; in the teachers colleges in the group, general education courses were used in 81 percent of the institutions. There do not appear to be any more recent figures available. See Robert A. Bullington, "Summary of a Study of College Science Courses Designed for General Education," in American Association of Colleges, *Bulletin,* XXXVI (1950), 267–72, and E. K. Weaver *et al.,* "Review of Recent Research in the Teaching of Science at the College," *Science Education,* XL (1956), 350–57.

[7] Bullington, p. 208.

[8] Nathan S. Washton, "A Survey of Science Courses for General Education in Colleges," American Association of Colleges, *Bulletin,* XXXIV (1948), 285–94.

[9] See Earl J. McGrath (ed.), *Science in General Education* (Dubuque, Iowa: William C. Brown Co., 1948), pp. 381–83, whence, unless otherwise credited, the descriptive material which follows has been drawn.

science on modern life—a story which cannot be told completely without referring on occasion to world affairs.[10]

How colleges go about giving science majors this understanding varies, but it is clear that courses which acquaint students with the historical development of science (as at Wesleyan), or which make extensive use of historical material (as at Antioch, Chicago, Colgate, Dartmouth, Louisville, and Chatham College) provide excellent possibilities for showing both the interdependence and interaction of scientific developments through the ages and all over the globe.[11]

Still other courses use philosophy to relate physical science to the story of Western culture, to other fields of human interest and activity, and to the problems our civilization faces today. These courses raise fundamental problems of cosmology, the nature and destiny of man, and the relation between science and religion.[12] They examine the interplay of scientific and humanistic ideas, and by showing how throughout history many non-scientific people have been affected by scientific ideas, they help cultivate a world view in their students. Even in courses which retain the approach of a single science, whether or not they reach out to bring in the materials of other sciences, as at Princeton or

[10] See Ordway Tead, "Effective Learning in College," *Journal of Chemical Education*, XXIX (1952), 565–70; Bullington, p. 270; and I. Bernard Cohen and Fletcher G. Watson (eds.), *General Education in Science* (Cambridge, Mass.: Harvard University Press, 1952), pp. v-xi by the editors, and the following contributions: Foreword, by James B. Conant, pp. xiii-xv; René J. Dubos, "Science and the Layman," pp. 3–15; Sidney J. French, "General Education and Special Education in the Sciences," pp. 16–33; and Philippe Le Corbeiller, "Applications of Science and the Teaching of Science," pp. 133–140.

[11] See I. Bernard Cohen, "The History of Science and the Teaching of Science," in Cohen and Watson, pp. 71–96; Leonard K. Nash, "The Use of Historical Cases in Science Teaching," in *ibid.*, pp. 97–118; and Frederick G. Kilgour, "Acquiring a Knowledge of the History of Science," in *ibid.*, pp. 119–30.

[12] Edwin C. Kemble, "The Role of Philosophy in a General Education Course in Physical Science," in *ibid.*, pp. 49–58; and Fletcher G. Watson *et al.*, "Science in the General Education Program at Harvard University," in McGrath, *Science*, pp. 99–102.

Oberlin,[13] it would be desirable to point out the international nature of the science. Some history departments (for example, at New York University) teach the history of science, and such courses can give both science majors and nonmajors who take them considerable insight into the true nature of science and its impact on civilization. Unfortunately, these courses reach too few people.

Mathematicians have apparently been even more reluctant than other scientists to provide undergraduates with materials and courses embodying the cultural background of their subject. For majors in mathematics, however, at least one such course is an essential part of their liberal education; for nonmajors, it is a valuable elective or possible alternative to the conventional beginning course in mathematics. A number of the colleges throughout the country (among them the University of Vermont, Bennington College, and the University of Buffalo) have, from time to time in recent years, presented courses setting out the cultural aspects of mathematics.[14]

Because basic developments in all the sciences have respected no national boundaries, it would not only reinforce instruction in world affairs, but give a truer picture of the nature of science and mathematics if instructors underlined for students the basically international character of their studies.[15] Including such material in courses would seem to be entirely possible in every

13 See Hubert N. Alyea, "The Single-Science Course at Princeton University," in McGrath, *Science,* pp. 124–39; Lloyd W. Taylor, "The Single-Science Type of Scientific-Appreciation Course," *ibid.,* pp. 185–93; and Earl J. McGrath, "Trends in Science Courses in General Education," *ibid.,* p. 384.

14 For an effective discussion of this problem, see Morris Kline, "Freshman Mathematics as an Integral Part of Western Culture," *American Mathematical Monthly,* LXI (1954), 295–306. See also his *Mathematics in Western Culture* (New York: Oxford University Press, 1953) and James R. Newman, *The World of Mathematics* (New York: Simon & Schuster, 1956).

15 "The University of Washington in World Affairs," *Universities and World Affairs,* Document No. 25 (Mimeographed; New York: Carnegie Endowment for International Peace, 1953), p. 4.

approach to the subject, historical, philosophical, case method, or in any combination of them. To a large extent, making clear the international aspect of science and mathematics is more a matter of the instructors' attitudes than of content. Most instructors in conventional science and mathematics courses do not consider that their courses can and should contribute to a student's understanding of world affairs.[16] If, however, they could all give the matter some thought, they would see that it is entirely possible for them to increase the students' awareness of world affairs without violating the essential purposes of their teaching.

[16] Only a minority of the reports in the "University and World Affairs" survey included courses in science among those contributing to an understanding of world affairs. On the other hand, at Gustavus Adolphus College, a combined faculty-graduate appraisal of courses in science showed that in that college a considerable amount of time was spent on the cultural achievements of other nations, current international problems, and the economic and political problems of other nations, as they came up in courses in biology, chemistry, geology, and physics. See "The Evaluation and Improvement of a Program of International Relations," *Universities and World Affairs*, Document No. 29 (Mimeographed; New York: Carnegie Endowment for International Peace, 1953), p. 2.

# CHAPTER SIX

# A Course in World Affairs

> From contemplation one may become wise, but knowledge comes only from study.
>
> A. EDWARD NEWTON, *A Magnificent Force*

A S THE PREVIOUS CHAPTERS have shown, the entire college curriculum can, if properly conceived, deepen a student's knowledge of world affairs. Nearly all faculty members can intensify a student's understanding of other fields as well as his own. This is not to say, however, that references by faculty members to subjects outside their specialties can replace instruction in those subjects. A philosopher's comments on physics are no substitute for physics, a physicist's discussion of sound no substitute for music, and a faculty awareness of international relations no substitute for instruction in world affairs.

Many colleges have come to believe since World War II that a course in world or public affairs is an important part of a liberal education. Some colleges which have already adopted such courses are Dartmouth, whose Great Issues course has been much publicized; Colgate, which requires every upperclassman to take a course in a foreign area and a course in America Confronts the World Community; Fisk; and Denver. The Dartmouth course[1] is

---

[1] See B. S. Bloom, "Course in Great Issues," *School Review*, LVI (1948), 439; Arthur M. Wilson, "Dartmouth's Venture in Great Issues," *Higher Education*, IV (1948), 209–10; and "Great Issues Course at Dartmouth College," *American Political Science Review*, XLIII (1949), 91–94.

avowedly an exercise in training more effective citizens. It tries to arouse in students a greater sense of public-mindedness and to make them more competent in using and evaluating the common sources of public information. The principal texts are the *New York Times* and the *New York Herald Tribune,* but the students also use official and semiofficial publications and periodicals. They read not only about the assigned issues, but in the first term prepare papers on the way the mass media cover the issues. The instructors assemble the materials that the students need for these projects in a Public Affairs Laboratory in the library and arrange exhibits to reinforce the classroom work. During the second semester, the students prepare papers on pressure groups and their role in public affairs, examining a particular group's constitution, history, activities, and publications. The Great Issues are usually stated in interdisciplinary terms, for example, Modern Man's Political Loyalties, The Scientific Revolution and the Radical Fact of Atomic Energy, International (and American) Aspects of World Peace, and Values for Modern Man. Guest lecturers usually speak on Monday evenings and are available on Tuesday mornings for question-and-answer periods. On Thursdays a faculty member gives the background of the topic which the next guest will present. The guest lectures with the subsequent question-and-answer period have proved extremely valuable, and have had a noticeable effect on the quality of campus "bull sessions." Whether the influence of the course extends into the lives of the alumni, the college is still attempting to determine. Not all the problems with which the Great Issues courses deal are in the realm of world affairs—the faculty selects "issues confronting the public-minded man . . . concerned with building . . . a sound economic order, the maintenance of a just peace, and the search for values which will enable our culture to survive"—but almost every issue has some international aspects, direct or indirect. Fisk University, although it is somewhat more dependent on campus lectures, has a similar course devoted to "problems or issues which condition thought or action in our time."[2]

Colgate requires each student in his junior or senior year to take a course in one foreign area (Britain and the Commonwealth, the Far East, Western Europe, Middle Europe, India and Southeastern Asia, the Mediterranean area, Latin America, or the Soviet Union). The university attempts, in these courses, to broaden the student's cultural perspective and to help him understand how problems in foreign lands arise from the area's physical environment, social structure and institutions, economic and political organization and activities, population composition and distribution, and mores and culture. In his last two years, every student also studies American Ideals and Institutions, where, *inter alia,* he compares and contrasts democratic ideologies with fascism and communism. He also takes the course entitled America Confronts the World Community, which is closely related to the other requirements and "stresses the place of American ideals and institutions in the international community and the consequence for our society of participation in this larger community."[3] The instructors and students attempt to determine how useful American ideas and procedures are for political leaders in other parts of the world; they study the views foreign observers hold of American democracy, examine American foreign policy, and analyze problems of international organization.

At the University of Denver, the Great Issues Seminar in Social Science, begun in January 1947, offers students an opportunity to bring their training to bear on crucial problems of society, for example: Soviet-American Relations, National Security, Freedom and Scientific Inquiry, Freedom and Education, and Freedom and Equality. The course, like its counterparts elsewhere, tries to create in students a continuing interest in and responsibility for participating in public affairs. Like the Dartmouth course,

2 *Fisk University Bulletin . . . Announcements for 1957–58,* p. 43.
3 *Colgate University . . . Catalogue 1957–58,* p. 71.

it provides for meetings with outside guests and conferences within and between departments.[4]     7 2 7 8 4

Colleges which do not already include such a course in the curriculum may want to consider very carefully those offered by Colgate, Dartmouth, Denver, and Fisk. Some faculties may quite reasonably decide that they are already teaching adequately about world affairs in social sciences or humanities courses. It is quite possible, for instance, that colleges, like Columbia College, with courses on Contemporary Civilization, where students now spend time discussing at least excerpts from the writings of Kautsky, Trotsky, Gandhi, Nehru, and Mao Tse-Tung and problems related to the United Nations, might conclude that they need no additional course. Other approaches to the subject, for example, those employed at the University of Chicago or in the Program of Integrated Liberal Studies at the University of Wisconsin may commend themselves to faculties. But even faculties which can honestly assure themselves that they are meeting the general students' need for instruction in world affairs will want to remain alert to ways of improving their offerings. Some may assume that they are contributing enough to a student's understanding of world affairs by teaching him how to search for truth and sound values and alerting him to the danger of propagandistic slogans in all walks of life. Or they may believe that by stressing the connections between world affairs and other fields— science, literature, sociology, politics, and economics—they are doing all they should to show how complex world affairs are. But even though a faculty does this much superbly, it would still be desirable for them to give a student some practice in applying to problems of world affairs the diverse elements of logic, fact, and value which the rest of his college training has given him. All the elements a student needs to understand something of world affairs may already be in the curriculum, but faculties cannot be

[4] *International Studies* (Denver: Social Science Foundation, n.d.), pp. 10, 15–17.

sure a student will know how to put the pieces of the puzzle together properly just because he has them before him. Students
need some experience in selecting and evaluating the vast amount
of data relevant to world problems.[5] The ability is not common,
for the ordinary citizen, when dealing with foreign policy matters, is only too apt to express his emotions and predetermined
opinions and indulge his personal preference rather than formulate considered views.[6] No one maintains that it is absolutely
impossible to develop skill even in conducting international relations without formal courses. But at the same time the fact that
college-trained men, and sometimes men in high places in government, have trouble overcoming their fancies in world affairs
argues that the ability to analyze these questions is not a natural
endowment and that colleges and universities can do much more
than they now do to help students respond rationally and re-
sponsibly to foreign policy problems.[7]

The conventional introductory course in international relations immediately suggests itself, if only as a matter of convenience, as a possible means of giving students this experience.
These courses in most cases survey systematically the elements of
national power, describe the state system and ways of conducting
foreign policy, touch on the basic principles of international law
and organization, and depict the foreign policies of the principal
states.[8] They are designed, however, like most conventional be-

5 For some cogent observations along this line, see Stephen Duggan, "The
Elements of Progress," Institute of International Education, *News Bulletin*
(New York), XX (Oct. 1, 1944), 3; "History, Politics and Foreign Affairs,"
*ibid.*, XX (Feb. 1, 1945), 4-5; "International Relations," *ibid.*, XX (May 1,
1945), 5.

6 See, for instance, Walter Lippmann, *The Public Philosophy* (Boston: Little, Brown & Co., 1956), especially chap. 2, for a thoughtful statement of this
problem.

7 Dorothy Fosdick, "Higher Education and World Affairs," in *Current Issues in Higher Education* (Washington: Association for Higher Education,
1955), pp. 18–25. See also Howard E. Wilson, *Universities and World Affairs*
(New York: Carnegie Endowment for International Peace, 1951), p. 36.

8 See *infra* for further discussion of the introductory course in international
relations, p. 113.

370.196

ginning courses, primarily for students planning to major in international relations; they tend therefore to set out superficially the material future specialists should later study in greater detail. As good as they may be for their purpose, they are not best suited for the general student, tomorrow's businessmen, physicians, lawyers, teachers, engineers, nurses, public relations specialists, or housewives.                                        SWi'

For the average man, world affairs come to his attention primarily in newspaper and radio reports. The intelligent American must evaluate these accounts because when he goes to the polls to choose representatives, senators, and a President, he bases his choices, at least in part, on the officials' position on questions of foreign affairs. The representative will have supported or condemned foreign aid; the senator will have criticized or praised the Foreign Service; and the President will have advocated containment, liberation, or some other policy which he may proclaim as a doctrine. One need only review the presidential elections of the twentieth century to see how issues of foreign policy have been thrust before the people. In 1900, for example, the Democrats under Bryan and Stevenson made imperialism the paramount issue, while the Republicans under McKinley and Roosevelt upheld the United States-built and -controlled Isthmian canal; in 1908 and 1912 tariff revision was a major issue between Taft and Bryan and later between Taft and Wilson; in 1916 the Wilson campaign dealt largely with neutrality and preparedness and the fact that Wilson had "kept us out of war," while Hughes's support from Irish- and German-Americans undoubtedly hurt him; the "solemn referendum" on the League of Nations probably ensured Cox's defeat in 1920; the tariff, World Court, disarmament, and the League of Nations figured in the 1924 campaign; the tariff and Philippine independence in 1928; the tariff and an international monetary conference in 1932; throughout the 1930's, United States neutrality was a critical issue, culminating in the 1940 election, where the national defense program, aid to

Britain, hemispheric defense, and foreign wars loomed large; in 1944, both political parties discussed a postwar international organization; in 1948, foreign aid and the United States role in postwar reconstruction were critical questions, and in 1952 Candidate Eisenhower's wartime role as Allied commander in chief and his "I shall go to Korea" speech helped defeat Stevenson even as the Hungarian uprising and Suez Canal crisis helped Eisenhower in 1956.

Because all the presidential elections since 1900 have involved questions of foreign policy, it is clear that the ability to analyze such problems is something every liberally educated American must have in order to make intelligent choices at the polls. The colleges and universities cannot ignore their responsibility to train young men and women whose opinions on world affairs will help shape the destiny of the United States and the world. And, of course, the opinions of educated citizens are important, not only at election time, but between elections, for highly emotional questions like foreign aid and recognition of Communist China force Congressmen, especially sensitive to public opinion, to assume attitudes which in part reflect the prevailing national temper. It is extremely important, therefore, that men and women holding influential positions in lawyers', doctors', veterans', and women's organizations, whose views Congressmen solicit, be able to make sound judgments on world affairs. They must not base their attitudes toward foreign affairs on prejudice, ignorance, myth, and fantasy. They must be able to understand how complex foreign policy is, to know why the leaders of the country do not always take the "obvious" solution and do not simply "wipe the Russians off the map" or "throw the Communists out of China."

Essentially the intelligent American college student needs to learn how the United States formulates and conducts its foreign policy, to consider all the complexities of arriving at decisions, to understand present directives, and to support or condemn them intelligently. The course best suited to help him play his role in world affairs is therefore one in United States foreign policy. Such a course will not give the citizen ready answers—in many cases, there are none—and certainly cannot solve for him problems that have not yet arisen, but it can help him acquire techniques for analyzing such problems and for judging independently the courses of action open to the United States.

In confronting the nation's foreign policy problems, he can use every bit of learning he has acquired in all his college courses: his psychology, his history, his languages, and his understanding of science. To the background information he has, he can add some understanding of current and, in many cases, long-range problems facing the United States and attempt to apply and analyze the available information about foreign policy problems in various parts of the world. He can learn how much information responsible officials need to develop foreign policies. He sees that to analyze foreign policy problems, he must know the history of an area and its politics and economics and understand the sociological and psychological complexities of the people with whom the United States deals. He learns how crucial it is to make careful assumptions about current situations and how dangerous misleading estimates can be. He learns how important it is to overcome biases and prejudices and revise one's views, if necessary, to make intelligent foreign policy decisions. Students of United States foreign policy will be forever alert to the prejudices that sometimes blind even statesmen to the consequences of their actions; they would know where to look for independent appraisals of foreign policy; they would know the value of seeing a situation from the "other side"; they would, in effect, have a laboratory experience in applying their knowledge to problems of survival. They will learn, moreover, to examine the consequences of their ideas.[9] An undergraduate, returning from the

---

[9] For a stimulating account of the value of such a course, see Fosdick, especially p. 23.

Korean War, is reported to have said to one of his teachers that he had discovered how much easier it was to study history than to make it. One hope of a required course in United States foreign policy is that it may confront students with real problems and thus help them make history better.[10]

A course in United States foreign policy can include lectures, reading, and discussions, but it lends itself superbly to various "model" techniques. In "model" courses, a type of sociodrama widely publicized in the Model United Nations sponsored by the American Association for the United Nations,[11] students assume in class the roles of members of responsible governmental organs. In this instance, the most apposite agencies would be the National Security Council or the Department of State.

A number of instructors are already using such techniques successfully. At the University of Michigan, for instance, as part of the course in The Foreign Policy of the United States, one instructor organized the entire class along the lines of a model "Department of State." The class was divided into model regional "bureaus" of the department, with each bureau headed by a graduate student—the course was open to both graduate and undergraduate students—as "assistant secretary," and the "offices" within each bureau by upperclassmen concentrating on specific areas.

The students in the regional offices of the Department of State met weekly outside of class; the entire bureau met fortnightly outside of class and in class every five weeks. In these meetings, students discussed some questions the instructor had prepared for them and other questions which arose spontaneously. At the end of the semester the bureaus produced reports summarizing

10 *Ibid.,* p. 25.

11 See R. E. Elder, "Teaching International Relations: Model Security Council or General Assembly," *American Political Science Review,* XLIII (1949), 95–98. For some elaborate exercises in "political gaming," see Lincoln P. Bloomfield, "Report and Analysis of Political Exercise, September 1958" (Hectographed; Cambridge, Mass.: Center for International Studies, Massachusetts Institute of Technology, 1958).

and evaluating contemporary American policy in the area and submitted their recommendations. The bureau chiefs also reported to the entire class before the course ended. Through this technique, the instructor brought source materials to the attention of students and gave each of them a chance to participate in a decision-making process under realistic conditions.

Quite a few instructors in courses in American foreign policy employ the "problem" approach, asking students to prepare "policy papers" along the lines of the Brookings Institution *Major Problems in American Foreign Policy*. In these papers, students set out objectives of United States foreign policy on some subject or toward some area, suggest alternative courses of action, and make their own recommendations for a policy. This approach has been used at Western Reserve University and the University of Utah, among others.

Through a course in United States foreign policy, a liberal arts college can best prepare students to discharge their responsibilities as citizens in the twentieth-century United States. Some colleges already have such courses in their curricula, or, if they do not, they may alter the content of a course they already offer to include the material of such a course, for instance, in the final sequence of a two-year social science course. But if a college does not offer this training in any form whatsoever, it should give serious thought to supplying it.

Whether to require such a course of all students is sure to be a serious problem for any college today, where existing schedules are already crowded. Giving students the kind of general education they need, seeing that they meet the prerequisites for their advanced work, instructing them in languages, and providing them with opportunities to explore the intellectual realm so as to discover their own interests—all of these demands at present fit only with the greatest difficulty into the undergraduate program. It is therefore difficult for faculties to decide to impose yet another required course on students, especially when the preprofessional needs of some (for example, in medicine) are already rigorous. A faculty should, however, consider a course in world affairs in relation to the entire curriculum. With adjustments throughout the college program, it might actually be possible to include a course in world affairs without increasing the number of courses students need to take.

Our look at the liberal arts student has shown us that study about world affairs should be an important part of the college curriculum; that existing courses in the humanities, social sciences, and natural sciences can, with few changes, contribute considerably to the total sum of a student's knowledge of world affairs; and that it is worthwhile for faculties to consider including, and perhaps requiring, in their curricula, a specific course in world affairs. With such opportunities available, students of any and all subjects can emerge as bachelors of arts, equipped, like their predecessors in other ages, to meet the challenges of their times. For those students who wish to specialize in world affairs, the college must make additional provisions, which we shall discuss in the next chapter.

# CHAPTER SEVEN

# World Affairs for the Major

The scholar is the student of the world; and of what worth the world is, and with what emphasis it accosts the soul of man, such is the worth, such is the call of the scholar.

EMERSON, "Literary Ethics"

A MAJOR IN WORLD AFFAIRS is by no means universally available in our colleges and universities. It is variously maintained that the subject is too professional, too superficial, or (paradoxically) too difficult for undergraduates. There seems to be ample evidence, however, that a world affairs curriculum can provide a good general background for the liberal arts students, that it can prepare future specialists well for graduate work in a number of fields, and that it need by no means be vocational education.

Some of the students who choose to study world affairs admittedly come to the subject for some vocational reason. They hope to enter their nation's Foreign Service or the Secretariat of the United Nations, join the staff of a corporation with international responsibilities, or become journalists in posts abroad—even as students of biology or chemistry may ultimately wish to be physicians; students of English to be advertising executives; and students of economics, securities analysts. It is, of course, wholly within the liberal arts tradition for colleges to give to all these students the background they seek for their professional work in medicine, business, or diplomacy, just so long as the faculty members teach in a spirit of exploration, discovery, and investigation.

Training the leaders of the professions is, as we have already seen, an age-old responsibility of colleges and universities, but despite the growing professionalism of the liberal arts colleges,[1] their special responsibility lies not in giving their students vocational skills, but in developing in them the capacity for leadership. A liberal arts college need not teach the future Foreign Service officer how to settle the estate of a deceased American any more than it must show the future economic analyst how to manage the pension fund of a large corporation, the future journalist how to file his copy, or the future advertising executive how to secure an account. A college must assuredly strive to help students build the scaffolding for their professional lives, but at the same time to educate them to be free men in the Renaissance tradition; beyond that, it cannot go. Rather than trifle with vocational minutiae, liberal arts colleges must try to develop in all future professionals the ability to acquire occupational skills and to apply themselves intelligently to whatever tasks may arise as they pursue their careers. They must graduate students who, though not skilled technicians, can equip themselves with further training to take a position or to serve useful apprenticeships on the job. Alert, intelligent, and able to grow, they are the persons who, as the leaders of American businesses and professions are rediscovering, make the best executives. Though there are jobs for holders of degrees from undergraduate schools in such fields as commerce, engineering, education, and even foreign service, the liberal arts colleges are not primarily concerned with training their students to take a place at once in the workaday world. The students may certainly have vocations in mind, but their hopes and ambitions do not taint the curriculum—they merely help the students draw from it what they want.

[1] See Earl J. McGrath and Charles H. Russell, *Are Liberal Arts Colleges Becoming Professional Schools?* (New York: Teachers College, Columbia University, 1958), especially pp. 17–20. For a provocative British commentary on related problems, see Sir Eric Ashby, *Technology and the Academics* (London: Macmillan Co., 1958).

In practical terms, it is difficult for colleges to draw the line between liberal and vocational education. Confusion has been compounded by the growing awareness that even in the traditional liberal arts subjects, advanced courses can be as specialized as any professional training in accounting or surgery. Senior seminars in the Irish renaissance, the history of Mexico, histological techniques and hematology, or microqualitative inorganic analysis are, to say the least, rather specialized, even though the English, history, biology, and chemistry departments offering them also offer courses which can expand the horizons of any nonspecialist. Contact with any field of intellectual activity can help liberate the mind of one unfamiliar with it; but in all subjects there is instruction so specialized as to be meaningless to the average intelligent person.

It is not true, on the other hand, as some have claimed, that any subject, properly taught, is liberal. A good teacher of carpentry, wise and humane, can give students a more liberal education than some teachers of Romantic poetry, but if he does so, it is because he has a noble spirit, not because carpentry itself is ennobling. Good teachers are always important, but some subjects, independent of their professors, contain within themselves seminal influences which can stimulate students to think or develop their powers of analysis and criticism, and others do not. If it is true that all subjects are liberal, some of them are undoubtedly more liberal than others,[2] and world affairs certainly belongs among the most liberal. Significantly enough, even those concerned with the undergraduate who wishes to enter the field professionally have not called for training that is vocational. At a meeting held in 1950 on the teaching of international relations, for instance, the conferees agreed on basic objectives indistinguishable from those of liberal arts colleges: to increase students'

[2] For a discussion of this question, see Harold K. Schilling, "What Should Be the Balance between Liberal and Specialized Education?" in *Current Issues in Higher Education* (Washington: Association for Higher Education, 1955), pp. 78–82.

knowledge, information, intellectual skills, range of interests, appreciation, and sensitivity; to improve their intellectual abilities, attitudes, and values; and to create greater consensus and cooperation among them.[3]

In general, instructors have taken two approaches in teaching world affairs to future professionals, but the two do not differ fundamentally, and both embrace the liberal arts. One group of academicians believes that students should prepare for careers in world affairs by taking as broad a liberal arts course as possible. The other group also favors giving students a broad background but prefers them to major in one of the social sciences. Sir Alfred Zimmern, for instance, in outlining a curriculum for undergraduates, urged them to elect courses in history, geography, foreign languages, physiology, psychology, history of science, sociology, and philosophy and to read works by Plato, Aristotle, Machiavelli, William James, Graham Wallas, Alfred North Whitehead, Lord Acton, and Oliver Wendell Holmes.[4] George Kennan also stresses the essentially wide range of understanding students of international affairs must have. He advises them to concentrate on the humanities: history, art, and literature.[5] Henry M. Wriston asserts that "the broader the acquaintance of the student with the fundamental disciplines in the humanities and the social sciences, the better equipped he is likely to be for understanding international problems."[6]

[3] Brookings Institution, International Studies Staff, *Report on a Conference on the Teaching of International Relations*, ([Washington]: The Institution, 1950), pp. 6–7. For an earlier view of the matter, which is entirely consistent, see Grayson Kirk, *The Study of International Relations in American Colleges and Universities* (New York: Council on Foreign Relations, 1947), pp. 22–23, 25–26.

[4] Zimmern, "International Understanding and the American College," in Sweet Briar College, *The Role of the Colleges in Promoting Peace through International Understanding* (Sweet Briar, Va.: The College, 1948), pp. 22–27.

[5] Address at the 39th Annual Mid-Winter Meeting of the National Alumni Association of Princeton University, Feb. 21, 1953, as printed in 83d Cong., 1st Sess., *Congressional Record*, XCIX, Part 9, Appendix, pp. A995–97.

[6] Wriston, "Education and the National Interest," *Foreign Affairs*, XXXV (1957), 579.

Those who wish students to major in one of the social sciences to prepare for a career in world affairs recommend that they study international law and organization, political and social theory, the problem of war, the emerging dependent peoples (imperialism and nationalism), and contemporary problems, and that they compare diverse national governmental institutions and ways of conducting foreign policies. But they also want students to take work in diplomatic history, United States foreign policy, comparative cultures, geography, economics, English and world literature, music, and fine arts.[7] Although this program emphasizes the social sciences, it also permits students to supplement their studies with extensive work in the humanities, and its advocates are by no means at opposite poles from those who favor the broadest possible education for students of world affairs.

It is hardly surprising that the champions of a broad liberal education for majors in world affairs differ among themselves about curricular details. They all agree, however, that no undergraduate interested in world affairs can, by the time he receives his bachelor's degree, explore all the subjects he needs or any one of them deeply enough to qualify as an expert. But colleges in our highly specialized world do not produce experts in any field whatsoever in four years. The inability to graduate as a certified statesman should not therefore deter students from studying world affairs in college. And for students not wishing to enter the field professionally, but wanting a good interdisciplinary liberal arts background, world affairs is also a worthwhile major.

But students should not proceed under any illusions. From the start the faculty should make it clear to the undergraduates that world affairs are complex, that studying them is no simple matter, that no one can substitute for concentrated study the attractive formulae and catchwords which publicists often use in talk-

[7] Howard Lee Nostrand and Francis J. Brown (eds.), *The Role of Colleges and Universities in International Understanding* (Washington: American Council on Education, 1949).

ing to or writing for the man in the street, that there is a great deal about the subject that experts themselves do not understand, and that it is a mistake to regard the subject as elementary. On the other hand, it is entirely feasible for faculties to give undergraduates the opportunity of studying world affairs. If students have the subject in their programs from the start, they can keep in mind its wide perspective in everything they study. They can bring together those portions of all their other courses which help them most to understand international relations, look at their curriculum from the "common angle" of which their courses will make them aware, and receive a liberal education which will most help them advance their special interests.[8] They will not know everything there is to know about world affairs by the time they get their degrees, but there is a midpoint between knowing nothing of a subject and knowing everything about it, "the midway position of one who knows enough at least to understand on precisely what points it may for a particular purpose be desirable to know more."[9] To help students, whether or not they plan to enter world affairs professionally, reach that midway position is a perfectly legitimate goal for colleges. As the student goes along in his work, he will not only learn much that will help him in his courses, but he will encounter a good deal that will excite him to probe ever more deeply into the economic, psychological, strategic, and historical subsoil of his subject.[10]

Despite a variety of approaches to world affairs, the college departments offering courses which may appropriately be regarded as the core subjects for the major are political science, economics, history, and languages, each of which we shall look at in

[8] For two informed discussions of the propriety of world affairs as an undergraduate study, see Zimmern, "Introductory Report to the Discussions in 1935," in *University Teaching of International Relations* (Paris: International Institute of Intellectual Cooperation, 1939), p. 11, and C. A. W. Manning (ed.), *The University Teaching of Social Sciences: International Relations* (Paris: Unesco, 1954), p. 18.

[9] Manning, p. 18.

[10] *Ibid.*, p. 19.

particular. As we have seen, nearly all college departments can contribute in some important way to a study of world affairs, and something more will be said about those which contribute especially to the interdisciplinary area programs. Finally, because programs in world affairs can succeed or fail depending on the way the college administers them, we shall have to say something else about administration.

## Political Science

Because it is the field in which international relations first came into its own, political science conventionally offers the largest group of subjects either required or recommended for majors in world affairs. Of its offerings, the most apposite are those in international relations, international law, international organization, and the foreign policies of the major powers (including the United States). In addition the political science departments offer political theory and comparative government, which are important to students of world affairs.

### Introduction to International Relations

Most colleges introduce students to world affairs through a political science course known under a variety of titles, usually some variation of Principles of International Politics. The prevailing view since World War II is that the first course in international relations should survey the field.

When, in 1947, Grayson Kirk wrote about teaching international relations, he found that the typical introductory course then offered dealt with five major topics: the nature and operation of the state system, factors affecting the power of the state, the international position and foreign policies of the great powers, the history of recent international relations, and the building of a more stable world order.[11] The course began by describing

[11] Kirk, pp. 27–29. Subsequent references to Grayson Kirk in this chapter refer to his views on pp. v and 27–31.

the nature and operation of the state system. It took up sovereignty, how the modern state system had evolved, how theories of state equality contrasted with the practices of unequal power politics, and the ways states conduct their relations with each other. The first task in this course was to examine the underlying principles and institutions of a multinational world; the last, to discuss the possibilities of developing international law and organization so that they might play a larger role in international affairs. The course paid considerable attention to the history of the League of Nations, the prospects for the United Nations, and the experience in setting up functional international organizations in the fields of health, education, labor, and dependent areas, among others. The individual instructors, according to their preferences, stressed either the centrifugal forces of power politics or the centripetal ones making for organized international cooperation.

A discerning person teaching such a course today could make it very meaningful. Few courses follow exactly the pattern Kirk described in 1947, however, partly because of the controversies over international relations provoked by the realists, partly because of the changed role of the United States in international affairs, partly because American scholars have changed their ideas about world affairs, and partly because of the growing amount of research in the behavioral sciences. The changes came gradually and had begun even as Kirk was writing. He based his analysis on the results of six regional conferences (organized by the Council on Foreign Relations in April and May, 1946) on teaching and research in international relations. When the conferees gathered, the world was just recovering from World War II. The International Court of Justice was organizing at the Hague and establishing its rules of procedure; the Russians had announced that they would withdraw their troops from Iran despite having vetoed the Security Council's resolution on the subject; the Nuremberg Trials were in progress; and the Paris

Peace Conference had begun. But the Truman Doctrine was still a year away. The United States was in the midst of what Winston Churchill has called a "deadly hiatus"[12] in its foreign affairs, still dominated by the postwar assumptions of great power unity enshrined in the United Nations Charter. There were admittedly some misgivings about Soviet behavior at the time—Secretary of State Byrnes had declared in February 1946 that the United States would not and could not "stand aloof" if force or the threat of force were used contrary to the purposes and principles of the United Nations Charter[13]—but official American opinion moved along in the spirit of postwar cooperation, and most college courses in international affairs reflected that spirit. Dispassionate observers of a world rebuilding itself could easily emphasize institutional arrangements, beginning with the nature and operation of the state system and ending with ways of building a more stable order. Whether optimistic or pessimistic, instructors selected their topics and arranged them in an order which implied that they believed that institutions would develop in time to govern world affairs. No matter how presented, a course which concluded with "building a more stable world order" inevitably raised in the student's mind, as the term came to an end, the problem of how best to organize the world along rational lines.

As Grayson Kirk's book came into being, however, the United States was becoming less optimistic about the possibilities of building an orderly postwar world along the cooperative lines envisaged during the war, at Dumbarton Oaks and at the San Francisco Conference. In March 1947 the Truman Doctrine was proclaimed, and in February 1948 the Soviet coup in Czechoslovakia occurred. The United States began to take a harder line toward the U.S.S.R. Soon the famous article setting out "The

[12] Winston S. Churchill, *The Second World War: Triumph and Tragedy* (Boston: Houghton Mifflin Co., 1953), VI, 455.

[13] Speech to Overseas Press Club, Feb. 28, 1946. See U.S. Department of State, *Bulletin*, XIV (1946), 358.

Sources of Soviet Conduct," signed by X (later identified as George Kennan) appeared,[14] and the United States policy of containment was under way. No longer was the United States a spectator, watching international politics at a distance; it began to participate very actively in events.

The changed perspective quickly found its way into the works of astute observers of the international scene like Hans Morgenthau, who in 1948 published his *Politics Among Nations,* followed in 1951 by his *In Defense of the National Interest* and by George Kennan's *American Diplomacy, 1900–1950.* The realists had set off their heavy artillery: power, which had received little attention from students of world affairs in the interwar period,[15] but which the United States had now begun to use consciously in world politics, started to get greater attention in introductory courses in international relations.

This change in accent had any number of subsidiary consequences. Where the courses immediately after the war had been largely historical and institutional, a concentration clearly evident in Kirk's five ingredients, they now began to pay more attention to theory and to the behavior of individuals and groups within the state that influence foreign policy decisions.[16] Instructors, whether they were realists or idealists, had to pay more heed to political theory than had been their custom, for they could protect their positions from erosion only by growing deep doctrinal roots. What the philosophers and political theorists had said about the nature of sovereignty, reason of state, democracy, freedom, power, and the prerequisites for successful international organizations and world peace assumed new importance. The actual power struggle in the postwar period stressed the

[14] *Foreign Affairs,* XXV (1947), 566–82.

[15] One exception was Frederick L. Schuman, whose *International Politics* (New York: McGraw-Hill Book Co., 1933) anticipated works to come.

[16] Forerunners of the behavioral school in writing about world affairs are Harold Lasswell, *World Politics and Personal Insecurity* (New York: McGraw-Hill Book Co., 1935), and Quincy Wright, *A Study of War* (2 vols.; Chicago: University of Chicago Press, 1942). See Waldo, especially chap. 5.

need for theory even more, as Communist ideology became a weapon in the battle for men's minds; one had to examine the effect of ideology on state behavior and inquire what antidote, if any, democracy could offer the uncommitted areas of the world against the powerful potions the Communists were dispensing.

Instructors in world affairs had always said something about power in their courses, but they began now to analyze its elements more thoroughly than ever before and to probe more deeply into the way states exercised their influence on the world scene. The commonly used phrase "United States as a world power" took on deeper meaning. Here again the debate between the realists and idealists was relevant because it raised issues of the propriety of various kinds of state behavior. Instructors had to describe the fundamental differences in the ways in which democracies and totalitarian states conducted their foreign affairs, determine the advantages and disadvantages of each, and look behind the mask of state behavior to find out who the actors on the international scene really were. The Nuremberg Trial decisions in 1948 had rejected the traditional doctrine that the agents of the state were not personally responsible for the way the state acted, and as controversial as the Nuremberg decisions were, they also forced students to identify the decision makers behind the anonymous spokesmen for the nations' foreign offices. Courses in world affairs consequently looked more at the ways states arrived at their policies; the pressures that operated on governments in fashioning their foreign programs; and the importance of élites, policy makers, and interest groups.[17] These approaches to world affairs called more attention to the materials of psychology and sociology as they related to the nature and behavior of groups and individuals in groups. As the instructors drew on fields other than politics for illuminating insights, they

[17] See, for example, Ernest B. Haas and Allen S. Whiting, *Dynamics of International Relations* (New York: McGraw-Hill Book Co., 1956), and the publications of the Foreign Policy Analysis Project, Organizational Behavior Section, Princeton, N. J.

tended to broaden even more than before both the theoretical bases of their courses and their interdisciplinary character.[18]

The emphasis on power had still another consequence for teachers of international relations. Some continued to build their courses to a climax, which culminated in a consideration of a stable world order, but others tended to treat international law and organization more as one part of the total picture of world politics or to subordinate them in deference to the indictment of legalism and moralism presented by Morgenthau and Kennan. The supporters of international law and organization reacted to the indictment by intensifying their search for stronger theoretical platforms of their own. All this activity tended to emphasize further the behavioral approach to politics as scholars attempted to determine the role of law and morality in world affairs and the effect of power politics on law and organization.

Concentrating on power, instructors also shook their courses in world affairs loose from any rigid conceptions of great and small states. Power is changing and dynamic, and looking to the ever-changing loci of power made it less difficult to meet the post-World War II need to direct students' attentions away from Europe to the potentials of Asia and Africa. The focus on power has also made it possible for instructors to pay more attention to military policy, military affairs, and strategic military concepts and has enhanced interest in environmental and capability analysis, that is, the ways in which the physical and human surroundings limit the options of decision makers.[19]

The five ingredients Kirk identified were in effect rearranged and embellished in the decade after 1947. Courses today stress power and the complexity of world affairs rather than the state system; they probe deeper into the elements of national power,

---

[18] See, for example, Charles P. Schleicher, *Introduction to International Relations* (New York: Prentice-Hall, 1954), and Vernon Van Dyke, *International Politics* (New York: Appleton-Century-Crofts, 1957).

[19] See, for example, Charles O. Lerche, Jr., *Foreign Policy of the American People* (New York: Prentice-Hall, 1958), pp. 16–22, especially notes 17–19.

and in so doing take account of the theoretical and practical results of research in economics, psychology, and sociology. In debating the position of the realists and idealists and presenting the cold war, instructors now pay more attention to theoretical presuppositions; and in presenting accurately the picture of world politics today, they have had to give a larger place than ever before to Africa and Asia.[20]

The courses in which colleges introduce international affairs are still eclectic, as they always have been. Few of them are purely institutional, historical, philosophical, or behavioral, for they tend to draw on all the social sciences for substance and approach. To be intelligently eclectic in such courses today is more difficult than ever before because of the growing volume of relevant data, but the students in the field are keenly aware of the challenge and meet it as best they can.

In teaching the courses in international relations, a number of instructors are using the case method to supplement lectures and general discussions. Widely used in law schools and since employed by other faculties, the case method is eminently suitable for courses in international relations which give increased attention to decision-making in foreign policy. Cases are extremely useful to give students specific information about events. They also help show how problems develop in international affairs and how the multiple facets of all problems interact. Cases heighten interest in a course and illustrate the process and dynamics of decision-making. The Brookings Institution did a great deal to demonstrate the efficacy of the technique in intro-

[20] I have drawn freely in writing about the changes in the course in international relations on Vincent Baker, "The Introductory Course in International Relations: Trends and Problems," *Universities and World Affairs*, Document No. 62 (Mimeographed; New York: Carnegie Endowment for International Peace, 1954), which is also cited and discussed in Norman D. Palmer and Howard C. Perkins, *International Relations* (2d ed.; Boston: Houghton Mifflin Co., 1957), p. xv. I am also indebted generally to the presentations in Vernon Van Dyke (ed.), *Some Approaches and Concepts Used in the Teaching of International Politics* (Iowa City, Iowa: State University of Iowa Press, 1957).

ducing its series *Major Problems of United States Foreign Policy*.[21] These problems delineated alternative national policies, which made them ideal for courses in United States foreign policy and adaptable for courses in international relations. Another series,[22] especially useful for courses incorporating material on the United Nations, was begun by the Carnegie Endowment for International Peace.

One example of how to use the case method effectively is found at Michigan State University; during the second half of Political Science 260, International Relations, the instructor requires each student to assume the role of "foreign minister" of a country other than the United States and the Soviet Union. The student must then review his chosen country's foreign policy toward both the U.S.S.R. and the United States during the past generation and must formulate a satisfactory foreign policy for the country in relation to the two superpowers for the next decade. The students start from the *Statemen's Yearbook* and then develop a bibliography for further reading. They must acquaint themselves with the possible biases of each author whose work they read (by examining his nationality, religion, politics, economic background, and education), and the instructor helps them consider the facts about "their" country's politics, psychology, sociology, economics, and strategy as well as the international relations between and among the country chosen and the two superpowers.

At Washington Square College, New York University, one instructor in a comparable course uses one historical problem to illustrate all aspects of the conventional course in world affairs. He takes advantage of the complete documentation available on the outbreak of World War I. Groups of students are made responsible for the source material relating to each of the seven

---

21 The series appeared annually from 1947 to 1954.

22 "United Nations Action" series. See Benjamin Rivlin, *The United Nations and Italian Colonies*, Case Histories: 1 (New York: Carnegie Endowment for International Peace, 1950).

powers (Austria-Hungary, France, Germany, Great Britain, Italy, Russia, Serbia) most directly concerned in the events leading up to the outbreak of the war, and at least once a week, the seven groups discuss the events which occurred between June 28 and August 3, 1914. Each group presents the "facts" from its own point of view and has the opportunity of seeing how the same events appeared from six other vantage points and how events elsewhere contributed to the crisis.

In order to use such techniques successfully, classes must be small enough for provocative discussion, of course, and the instructor must prepare or procure appropriate materials. It is particularly difficult to take up current problems through the case method unless the instructor has unusual facilities available and a great deal of time to prepare the cases. Instructors interested in these techniques now have available at least two compilations of cases suitable for analysis in introductory courses,[23] but to use the case system from year to year on current problems, would require a staff equipped to prepare background papers on a continuing basis.[24]

It is quite customary for instructors of international relations to require term papers of one sort or another from their students, either as assigned additional reading or research topics worked out individually with the student. At Western Reserve University an instructor in a course in Principles of International Politics has tried to help his students to develop their ability to interpret what they read and to think critically about it by giving them a prescribed format to use in analyzing four articles they select from the learned journals on international affairs. He gives them a list of the journals and adjures them to evaluate the articles they select to determine how important the problems discussed

[23] Andre Gyorgy and Hubert L. Gibbs, *Problems in International Relations* (New York: Prentice-Hall, 1955); and Elton Atwater *et al., World Affairs: Problems and Prospects* (New York: Appleton-Century-Crofts, 1958).

[24] For an analogous series, see the cases in the Eagleton Foundation Series of "Case Studies in Practical Politics" (New York: Henry Holt & Co., 1958).

are, how adequately the author treats the problems, how original his thesis is, and how competent he is to handle his subject. The students are then asked to analyze the articles (1) to determine the author's basic assumptions about the nature of man, society, power, morality, and the way these elements relate to each other; (2) to identify and illustrate with selected quotations the author's central and subordinate theses; (3) to determine the author's views of the "national interest," the objectives of policy, the power necessary to bring the policy into being, and the risks in carrying it out; (4) to look for evidence of consistency or inconsistency, fallacies in presentation, and the degree to which the author recognizes both the complexity of the problem he is discussing and the consequences of his recommendations; (5) to compare the author's views with those of other standard authorities and determine whether the differences are in facts, conceptions, or evaluations; and (6) to assess the actual value of the author's thesis to a policy maker or practical politician. The instructor hopes that by assisting students to analyze their reading, he will help them develop their own view of international relations which will assist them after college in making more valid and meaningful interpretations of international politics.

Over the years, the introductory course in international relations has quite clearly maintained the elements included in it after World War II. Instructors have modified it, however, to take account of the battle between the realists and idealists, of the growing interest in power, and of the behavioral approach to the social sciences. New teaching methods, such as are involved in using cases, have also arisen out of the emphasis on decision-making. The course will undoubtedly continue to change in response to new developments in the social sciences.

## INTERNATIONAL LAW

Before international relations assumed its central role in the study of world affairs, the dominant subject was international law, but international law lost considerable prestige in the years between the two world wars. Both the general public and scholars became discouraged by the small part law seemed to play in the affairs of states. The tendency to discount the law was accelerated by the initial impact on the teaching of world affairs of the realists who seemed ready to give the subject its *coup de grâce*. Pushed to the wall by events inside and outside the academic community, which made it increasingly difficult to maintain a separate course in international law for undergraduates, the teachers of the subject took a closer look at their material. Some, at least, are now moving to close the gap between theory and practice, so apparent in the work of the theorists who maintain that international law exists as a series of rules with a life independent of state behavior.[25] Just as the tendency to divorce international law from politics may have driven students away from studying the law, the new attempts to integrate our constantly growing knowledge about international politics with the traditional doctrines of the law may bring them back. The realists who came to bury the law may have done its students a great service by jarring them loose from theories unrelated to facts and may help them ultimately to assess the normative elements of their study. Teaching international law is important in college programs of world affairs because within the law are the inspirational ideas which alone can raise the conduct of international affairs out of the jungle. The civilizing ideas of law and order are slow to operate, but it is important to preserve them as positive forces which may generate social and political change.

[25] Cf. Hans Kelsen, *General Theory of Law and State* (Cambridge, Mass.: Harvard University Press, 1946) and *Principles of International Law* (New York: Rinehart & Co., 1952), with Charles de Visscher, *Theory and Reality in Public International Law,* trans. Percy E. Corbett (Princeton, N.J.: Princeton University Press, 1957) and Percy E. Corbett, *The Study of International Law* (New York: Doubleday & Co., 1955). See also "Conference on the Teaching of International Law," *American Journal of International Law,* LI (1957), 92–94, and Paul de Visscher, "Conference on the Teaching of International Law," *The Yearbook of World Affairs, 1957* (London: Stevens & Sons, 1957), pp. 257–72.

It would be a mistake to cut undergraduates off from the only stuff of which a future world order can be built (if it can ever be built at all).[26]

Teachers of international law in colleges today are more concerned than ever before with jettisoning unreality. The beginning course in international law, for instance, usually takes up what was once called the Law of Peace. It leaves for legal specialists the Law of War, dealing with the laws of warfare, enemy property, neutral rights and duties, and belligerent interference with enemy and neutral commerce at sea (prize law), all of which once received equal attention with the Law of Peace. The first course in international law now conventionally attempts to define international law and show what is meant by the family of nations; and tries to relate international law to municipal law, history, political theory, and philosophy. The course also takes up such topics as the subjects of international law, recognizing states and governments, nationality, territory of states, state jurisdiction, succession, diplomatic intercourse, and treaties and agreements. It may also examine the problems of war crimes and the role of the United Nations in collective security.

To keep their courses as meaningful as possible a number of instructors bring into them contemporary legal controversies which illustrate some of the legal principles the students are discussing. With the United States so actively involved in international politics, such issues are numerous, and instructors have been quick to capitalize upon student interest in the problems of recognizing Communist China, evaluating the Japanese claims upon the United States for the injuries United States hydrogen bomb tests caused to some Japanese fishermen, applying the status-of-forces agreements in Europe and Japan, determining the law which applies in the controversies over the Gulf of Aqaba

26 See, on this point, Quincy Wright, "The Teaching of International Law in the Postwar World," *Proceedings of the Eighth Conference on the Teaching of International Law and Related Subjects* (Washington: Carnegie Endowment for International Peace, 1946), pp. 22–28.

and the Corfu Straits, and interpreting treaties relating to the Suez Canal controversy. Nuclear power and space satellites have propelled man into new worlds of legal problems whose solutions are at present as dimly seen as the promises and threats the new technological advances hold for man. Wrestling with the legal difficulties which they pose—the sovereignty of space and the safeguards against diversion of atomic materials from peaceful to military purposes, for instance—is a vital and exciting exercise for any group of students.[27] Instructors have also helped students appreciate the immediacy of legal problems by catering to their regional interests, for instance, by allowing undergraduates in the Pacific Northwest to go into the status of the territorial sea as it relates to offshore oil, international fishing rights, and disputes between the United States, on the one hand, and Canada and Mexico, on the other.[28]

Instructors have a good many textbooks available to use in undergraduate courses in international law, although many instructors illustrate the principles discussed in the texts by having students read selected cases. There are excellent casebooks available also, but most of them are prepared for the wide but more specialized markets of the law schools. Cases properly presented provide more of a challenge than textbooks in introducing international law to undergraduates, but casebooks available today seem too formidable to many undergraduates. Instructors need a book of readings in international law that includes leading cases, a book that would be analogous to the small casebooks

[27] For preliminary explorations of these problems, see *Proceedings of the American Society of International Law* (Washington: The Society, 1956, 1957, and 1958).

[28] Illustrations of this kind have been widely used all over the country, in courses, for instance, at Tulane University, the University of Minnesota, the University of Washington, and New York University. See also Charles E. Martin, "The Teaching of International Law from the Viewpoint of Political Science Programs, Graduate and Undergraduate," in University of Washington Institute of International Affairs, *Bulletin*, No. 12 (July 1954), mimeographed, p. 5.

which have long existed in constitutional law.[29] Such a book might do a good deal to make the teaching of international law more feasible in courses in international politics and might even help to stimulate interest in more full-semester courses in international law than now exist in colleges.

INTERNATIONAL ORGANIZATION

The founding of the League of Nations gave rise to courses in international organization, which first appeared in the curriculum of American colleges in the 1920's. Research and study waxed and waned with the fortunes of the League, but with the formation of the United Nations and the establishment of its headquarters in New York, American interest in the subject intensified.

Few specialists now regard international organizations as preludes to Utopia, as they once did.[30] They see them rather as institutions which social scientists should study systematically with the best available tools. Some colleges give International Organization as a course in the second semester of a two-semester offering where the first semester is in International Law (Carleton College); some combine it in a course entitled International Organization and Administration (University of Washington), but most often colleges offer it as a one-semester course by itself. Whether formally connected with instruction in law or administration or not, both subjects inevitably enter the course, along with international politics, since one cannot isolate the United Nations from international law, administration, and relations.

Instructors in international organization now concentrate on the United Nations as once they did upon the League. Nearly all of them study the United Nations and its several kinds of activities: political, economic and social, legal, administrative, and its care for dependent peoples. They usually begin by examin-

29 This need was noted by Martin, p. 7, and the writer shares his view most emphatically.
30 See Kirk, pp. 37–39.

ing the background of international organization (the League and some of its predecessors as far back as the Rhine Commission) and end by theorizing about the future of international organization as a way of conducting international affairs. At some point, they also give some attention to the specialized agencies of the United Nations and regional organizations not connected with the United Nations. They also take account of the policies of the member states in the United Nations, about which more and more material is becoming available.[31]

At New York University, where the model technique has been used extensively, the students have available a collection of United Nations documents virtually as complete as that of the United Nations itself. But the technique has also been used in colleges where the library can arrange to purchase regularly a few basic documents like the *Yearbook of the United Nations,* the *Annual Report of the Secretary-General,* the reports of the Assembly committee in whose jurisdiction falls the particular problem to be taken up in class, and any special reports dealing with the problem itself. Because of the very nature of the model technique and the fact that debates are to be simulated, every student should have a copy of the *Rules of Procedure of the General Assembly,* a very inexpensive publication available from the U.N.

Similar approaches have been used by the Woodrow Wilson School of Public and International Affairs of Princeton University in their undergraduate conferences and at Emory University, where students in a course in international organization undertook at one time to study the United Nations Charter review.

FOREIGN POLICY

A course in United States foreign policy, which has been recommended in chapter 6 as most appropriate for the general student of world affairs, is also important for the undergraduate major.

[31] See the "National Studies on International Organization" series published by the Carnegie Endowment for International Peace.

As offered at present in most colleges, this course now takes up United States foreign policy in diverse areas of the world, looking at each in turn. It also generally includes introductory material, theoretical in nature, touching on power politics and the diverse approaches of realists and idealists to foreign policy; some historical background; material on the way the United States conducts its foreign policy; and refers as well to domestic influences on foreign policy. Just how much attention instructors give to these problems in foreign policy courses depends in large part on the other courses available to students. For instance, those colleges which offer separate courses in the conduct of foreign policy pay less attention to this subject.

## Economics

No student of international relations can secure a well-rounded picture of world affairs without knowing how economics affects international tensions. A world in which the United States must choose between pumping dollars into the Japanese economy and shutting its eyes to Japanese trade with a mainland Chinese regime the United States does not recognize, in which Communist parties can exploit illiteracy and poverty in Latin America and Asia among people who feel that the United States does not sufficiently sympathize with their economic objectives, in which Europeans are generating new political power by uniting in a Common Market—such a world requires those who study it to pay considerable attention to economics.

Economics departments traditionally offer courses in international economics for their own majors, and such courses inevitably include technical matters of less interest to students of world affairs. To accommodate the international relations major, therefore, the University of Denver has created a special course called The Economics of International Relations which examines the economic bases of international relations, the growing impact of the United States on the world economy, and the stake of the

United States in world economic prosperity. The University of Chicago offers a similar course in Economic Aspects of International Politics. Such specially designed courses represent a very desirable approach to the problem of economics for the international affairs major, but one which is, of course, feasible only in large universities. Where such special courses are not available, it is always possible to pay more attention to politics in courses in international economics, a trend which indeed is visible in a number of institutions.[32] The instructor of the course at Michigan State University, for example, orients his course around questions of public policy—the course itself is called International Economics and Public Policy—and examines international economics in terms of policies that restrict trade and those which enhance it. His approach relates the economic and political implications of the questions the students consider and consequently makes the course much more meaningful to students of world affairs (and probably even for students of economics) than it would otherwise be. The International Economics courses at Western Reserve University and Reed College employ a historical approach to the economic policies of the United States and other nations, and inevitably relate national economic policies to politics. At Emory University, the instructor's approach is avowedly that of "political economy," and correlates the economic and political views of theorists like Alexander Hamilton and John Locke.

No matter what attention economists give to political matters in their courses, many subjects with which they must deal are by nature technical. One cannot effectively learn or teach about cartels, exchange and import controls, tariffs, commodity agreements, dollar shortages, and balances of payments and exchange without acquiring a technical vocabulary. As a result, it is customary to allow students to take up international economics only after introducing them to economics in general and giving them

[32] See Kirk, p. 41, for a discussion of this problem.

some background in money and banking. However, there is no unanimity about how much technical background the student of world affairs or of economics must have to take up international economics. Students in the Department of Foreign Affairs at the University of Virginia, for instance, must first take two two-semester courses in Principles of Economics and Money and Banking before they can take the required six semester-hours in international economics.

The University of California (Berkeley), which also requires its majors in international relations to take a two-semester course in international economics, has them precede it only by a two-semester course introducing them to economics. The Woodrow Wilson School of Public and International Affairs at Princeton does not require students to take International Trade and Finance, and, although the university designates the course for upperclassmen only, those who take it have no prerequisite to meet. They can acquire the background they need in two semesters by taking two one-semester courses in The Structure and Functioning of the National Economy and Money and Banking. They can, however, take International Trade and Finance without any preliminary work in economics. Presumably those without any preparation must work harder than their confreres, but the obstacles are not insuperable.

There are, it is clear, institutions which have found it possible to give to their students of world affairs work in international economics which neither distorts the focus of their study of world tensions nor unbalances their entire curriculum by requiring them to take so many courses in economics that they do not have the opportunity to study in other departments.[33] If colleges introduce students to economics during their first two years of work, it would seem entirely feasible for world affairs majors to

[33] For a thoughtful approach to this problem, see Klaus Knorr, "Economics and International Relations: A Problem in Teaching," *Political Science Quarterly,* LXII (1947), 552–68.

include in their program without difficulty at least one (and probably two) semesters in international economics. If their minimal preparation for the course in international economics is technically deficient in any way, they should be able to make up the deficiency by judiciously selected supplemental reading.

## *History*

The more history the major in international relations knows, the better equipped he is to understand today's tensions. The amount of history students should study as part of their major depends on what they know by the time they begin concentrating. The present consensus is that they should know American history, modern European history ("modern" in this case going back at least to 1648), and the diplomatic history of the United States. Beyond this minimum, colleges ordinarily permit them to decide what history to study, according to their special interest. For instance, Russian history and Far Eastern history are obviously desirable for students interested in the great power struggle today; Latin American history, for those primarily concerned with the neighbors to the south; and the history of the Commonwealth countries, for many purposes.

The University of California (Berkeley) requires either European or American history as a prerequisite for the major and then urges students to include additional history in their programs. At Princeton, the university requires all students to complete two history courses (in political, economic, and cultural history; history of scientific thought; or the history of ideas as reflected in religious and philosophical ideas). In addition, the Woodrow Wilson School at Princeton requires its students to select history courses which will give them a good grounding in American and European history and American political institutions, and makes seven history courses available to its majors in international affairs. These majors could under the university's written rules make up a program without including an additional history course beyond the required minimum, although it is quite unlikely that any adviser would approve such a program, and it would be extremely difficult to pass the departmental general examinations in the junior and senior years without knowing some history. At the University of Chicago, where the College requires all students concentrating in the social sciences to take two year-long sequences in the development of civilization (the history of Western civilization, the development of American civilization, or the development of non-Western civilization), the Committee on International Relations requires its majors to complete whichever one of the three they have omitted in their core work. Colgate requires all its international affairs majors to take American History since 1865 and American Foreign Relations. Majors at Colgate, although they need not take any history beyond that required of all students, may select from two to five additional history courses.

Programs for international affairs majors at Syracuse, Virginia, and Denver also use this approach: they do not require students to include history in their programs, but it is always available as one possible option, or it is highly recommended.

## Languages

Although requirements differ, all the major programs in American universities emphasize how important languages are. The University of Denver does not require students to take any specified language courses, but it does insist that they demonstrate a reading and speaking ability in at least one foreign tongue. California requires its majors to study fifteen units of language beyond the four-unit beginning course for French, German, and Spanish or a total of fifteen units of Russian, Chinese, Japanese, or Portuguese and gives majors a special departmental reading test. Syracuse and the University of Chicago require two years work in one language; Virginia, four. Colgate, which exempts students from studying a foreign language in college if they meet certain examination requirements (including an oral examination given by the university), requires other students to study a foreign language for two years and suggests that *(a)* students planning to take the Foreign Service Examination elect three years of work in a single language, and *(b)* those planning to attend graduate school elect two years of work in each of two languages. For languages not offered by the university, they arrange for students to take intensive summer courses at other universities. There seems to be no tendency on the part of any of the universities to allow majors in world affairs to slight foreign languages, an emphasis which is entirely logical and proper.

## Other Subjects

Few programs for majors in world affairs require students to study any subject outside of history, economics, politics, and languages, and beyond these subjects, they are far from unanimous in their requirements. The divergence arises from differing conceptions of what is proper, from varying interests of the students, and from the courses available in the various colleges and universities. Nearly all, however, call students' attention to courses in geography, sociology, and anthropology, when they are available. Colgate, for instance, requires its students to take either political or economic geography (offered by its Geography Department) and either an introductory course in sociology or anthropology. All the programs show that the faculties are aware that a student interested in world affairs cannot achieve his objectives by studying in only one field or learn all he needs to know about all fields related to world affairs. The programs do, however, permit the majors to start along the road to competence and show him how complex world affairs can be.

A number of colleges and universities offer regional specialties for undergraduates, among them the University of California (Berkeley), Syracuse, Colgate, Western College for Women, and San Francisco State College. The University of California (Berkeley), has one of the largest of these programs, for it permits undergraduates to major in East Asia, China, France and French Colonies, Germany and Central Europe, Hispanic America, Japan, Russia and Eastern Europe, and Southeast Asia. The prerequisites for each of these programs differ, but nearly all ask students to take a course in the history of the area before they enter their major and to undertake a study of the principal language of the area as their work proceeds. In addition to the history prerequisite, the students must also take two semesters' elementary work in one or, more often, two related fields of study, usually in art, anthropology, economics, geography, or political science. The regional major then consists of twenty-four to thirty units of work selected from as many as eight departments. Thus a major in Japan might select from courses in anthropology, art, economics, geography, history, Oriental languages, political science, and sociology.

Students at Syracuse may study in five geographical areas: England and the British Commonwealth, Western Europe, Russia and the Soviet Union, the Far East, and Latin America. Here, students do not spread their work as widely as they may at California (Berkeley), because they may take only twelve hours of work in each of the areas along with twenty-one hours of basic courses in international relations. No area includes courses from fewer than four of the participating departments: Anthropology, Economics, Geography, History, Philosophy, Sociology, and the various language and literature departments. Syracuse also permits students to group their courses into functional specialties, Comparative Systems of Political Economy (in which students may study in economics, geography, philosophy, political science, and sociology), Economic Resources and Foreign Trade (economics, finance, geography, and marketing), and Peoples and Cultures (anthropology, geography, psychology, and sociology).

Colgate offers area studies in Asia, Britain and the Commonwealth, Latin America, Western and Central Europe, Russia, and the United States. Students are all required to take a special Area Studies Seminar, and in addition at least three courses on the area, selected from specified offerings in the Departments of Economics, Geology, Geography, History, Religion, and in several literature departments; and two courses from either those departments or several others: anthropology, sociology, philosophy, psychology, and political science. A student at Colgate could make up a program consisting of courses from ten departments, although it is unlikely that many do so. Colgate also permits its students, as part of their major in international affairs, to arrange for sequences in diplomatic history, international economics, or political geography, in which they might take as many as five courses in geography, or four in history and economics, in addition to the prerequisites in those subjects.

Western College for Women has provided a good example of how a small college can include work in specific areas in an interdisciplinary program in Intercultural Studies. Students concentrating in this program take five courses—or their equivalent in independent work—from a selected list in art, economics, education, intercultural studies, music, philosophy, political science, religion, and sociology. In addition, the college specifies that all majors must take twenty-three semester hours in Intercultural Studies: The Development of World Civilization (a six-semester-hour course, incidentally, which the college now requires all its students to take); Social and Economic Geography; a special senior Integrating Course; and twelve semester hours in Contemporary Civilization, the most unusual feature of this program. This Contemporary Civilization course is conducted on a four-year cycle, treating the economic, political, social, religious, and educational institutions and movements of a different geographical area (Europe, Latin America, the Middle East, and Asia) each year. It is one of two courses normally offered by a visiting professor from the area. (The other presents the history of the area.) Students must take the Contemporary Civilization course twice (that is, in two areas) as part of their programs.

The Western College program, albeit neither so broad nor so flexible as those in larger institutions, is a bold, imaginative attempt to fulfill the college's announced objective of presenting the world's major systems of culture and encouraging "through the shared experiences of international life on the campus general attitudes of goodwill toward all men and appreciation of the values of all civilizations." The college seems to have made a good start in providing its students from many countries "with fundamental knowledge of world community, world problems, and world peace, and with the necessary background and appreciation for world travel."[34]

Another ingenious approach to area studies was taken in St. Paul, Minnesota, where the Colleges of St. Catherine and St. Thomas, Macalester College, and Hamline University, have, since 1953, cooperated through the Hill Center of Area Studies to provide an integrated area-study program for upperclassmen in all four institutions. The geographical emphasis of the program changes annually in a three-year sequence, which includes the Far East, the Middle East, and the Soviet Union. Each year, the Hill Center provides an eight-semester-hour interdisciplinary course of study on one area of the world. For instance, every third year, the Far Eastern program, emphasizing China and Japan, considers the impact of Western civilization on the area and the significance of the Far East in contemporary world affairs, as well as the education, geography, art, literature, philosophies, and religions of the area.

Ten students from each college may enroll in the course, and the eight instructors (two from each college, varying from year to year, depending on the area being studied) come from the departments of economics, education, geography, history, literature, philosophy, political science, and sociology. The Hill Foundation

---

[34] *Western College Bulletin, 1957–1958* [pp. 8–9]; see also *infra* for supplementary summer travel seminar, pp. 159–60.

makes it possible for each instructor to spend the summer preceding his teaching preparing for his course through study, research, or travel. Coordinating the programs of the four institutions to make these courses possible has been a difficult, but not an insuperable, task, and each year one of the eight instructors has served as coordinator.

Whether the program, which would not have been possible without foundation support, can continue is uncertain, but it has without doubt provided an important example of what colleges and foundations can accomplish through cooperation.[35]

San Francisco State College also shows how liberal arts colleges can create a rich major in area studies from their regular curricula if they have sufficient imagination to permit students to cross disciplinary lines. A major in international relations there may concentrate in an area after taking four or five courses in international relations. If he chooses the Far East, for example, he may select at least six courses from a list including Peoples and Cultures of the World, World Population Problems, Economics of Underdeveloped Areas, Geography of Eastern Asia, European Imperialism, Asian Nationalism, United States Diplomatic History, History of the Far East, United States Foreign Policy, Contemporary Far East, Race and Ethnic Relations, Far East from World Business Viewpoint, History of Chinese Painting, Exotic Music, Oriental Literature and Life, and Religions of Mankind. In all, eleven departments cooperate in making these courses available. Students wishing to focus their area work on the U.S.S.R., Western Europe, the Middle East, or Latin America have similar opportunities.

It is therefore entirely possible for colleges to work out programs which give the student both solid grounding in the core subjects and the opportunity to indulge a special interest with-

[35] Asia Society, "Asian Studies in Undergraduate Education" (Mimeographed; New York: The Society, 1957). See also Ward Morehouse, *Educational and Cultural Activities on Asia: An Account of Recent Developments in the United States* (New York: Asia Society, 1958), pp. 10–11.

out sacrificing the broad understanding appropriate to the liberal arts.[36] No student graduating from any of these programs would be an area specialist in the sense of his graduate counterpart, but that is neither desirable nor expected. If he goes on to further work, he will know how to proceed, and may broaden or narrow his program as necessary; if he terminates his formal education with his bachelor's degree, he will have a solid core of courses no liberally educated man need be ashamed of.

## Integrating Devices

Because the majors in world affairs must study so many diverse subjects, it is extremely important for colleges to help them bring their knowlege in diverse fields to bear on world affairs. Some instructors, by their own broad approach to their subjects, will undoubtedly assist their students to relate the various fields of knowledge, but since most college courses are by their nature multipurpose, colleges need to make special arrangements to help students of world affairs integrate their work.[37] The devices colleges may employ are not secret, and are already in use in a num-

[36] Deming Brown, "A Report on the Undergraduate Russian Area Programs of Nine American Universities" (mimeographed) gives a detailed analysis of multidisciplinary undergraduate majors in Russian Studies at the University of California at Berkeley, Dartmouth College, Fordham University, Indiana University, University of Michigan, Stanford University, Syracuse University, University of Washington, and Yale University. For other interesting interdisciplinary programs, see Asian and Inter-American Studies Programs at Florida State University; the Foreign Studies Program at Michigan State University (China, Latin America); the University of Michigan (Far East, Near East, and Russia); the University of Minnesota (Scandinavian Area Studies, Northwest Europe, Russia, East and South Asia, and Latin America); Stanford University (Hispanic-American Studies Program and the Pacific-Asiatic and Russian Programs); Roosevelt University (Africa, Western Europe, Central Europe, and Eastern Europe); the University of Texas (Latin America and Eastern Europe); the University of Washington (Far East and Russia); the University of Wisconsin (East Asian Studies, Hispanic Studies); Yale University (Chinese, Japanese, Russian, and Southeast Asia Studies).

[37] For an excellent discussion of the theoretical and practical problems of integrating studies of areas and world affairs, see Hans J. Morgenthau, "Area Studies and the Study of International Relations," *International Social Science Bulletin,* IV (1952), 3–11.

ber of institutions—tutorial or preceptorial systems as at Harvard and Princeton, and comprehensive examinations in use at these institutions and at Dartmouth, Cornell, Columbia, Brown, Ohio Wesleyan, Swarthmore, Reed, Grinnell, Lehigh, Lafayette, Kenyon, Rochester, the University of Pennsylvania, Yale, Haverford, and others. Another useful device is to require students to write an undergraduate thesis or honors essay, a system used at Harvard, Princeton, the University of Chicago, and the University of Wisconsin, among others. Seminars especially for students in world affairs, such as the honors seminars at the University of Rochester, the Asia Studies Seminar at Colgate, the senior seminars at San Francisco State College and the University of Texas, the interdisciplinary faculty seminar at the Far Eastern Institute of the University of Washington, may also be used to help students of world affairs tie together the various strings of their courses and think across departmental lines.[38] The greater emphasis educators have begun to place upon freeing students from formal course requirements will also provide creative faculties with excellent opportunities for arranging interdisciplinary studies in world affairs.

The undergraduate conferences at Princeton's Woodrow Wilson School of Public and International Affairs provide students with excellent opportunities to use their knowledge in studying and solving cooperatively problems of public policy, domestic and international. The conferences give students experience not only in investigating concrete political or economic problems, but also in presenting their findings, both orally and in writing, and making decisions by democratic processes.

The faculty conference director prepares a syllabus, which states the problem for the students to investigate (for example: U.S. Policy in Western Europe: Next Phase; Security of the American Worker; The U.S. and the World's Food Supply; and American Aid Policies in the Near East). He provides a schedule

[38] See Kirk, pp. 49–51.

of course meetings and a basic list of required and suggested readings, and suggests how best to cover the material. At this point, the students take over the primary responsibility for organizing the conference and undertaking the necessary research. They group themselves into "commissions" to study different aspects of the problem, each member of a commission investigating a different issue.

Their final papers contain one-sentence statements of the problem, two or three pages summarizing the principal findings of fact, one to four pages of policy implications and recommendations, and a discussion of at least twenty pages. The conference director and a member of the Department of English then criticize the paper. Meanwhile, the school brings specialists to the campus to address the conferees, and the conferees take field trips to interview experts whose advice they need. During the last month of the semester, they hold their formal conference sessions, hear reports from each member, and, working through their commissions, hammer out actual policy recommendations.[39]

These conferences—the school offers two each semester, and requires students to take three during their upper-class years—are excellent teaching and learning devices of proven value which deserve to be copied and adapted by other colleges throughout the country.

## *Administrative Arrangements*

Where colleges offer world affairs as a major field of study for undergraduates, they do so in three ways. They may establish a separate department or school to supervise instruction; they may permit several departments to offer an interdepartmental major; or they may offer international relations as a major field within one department. Just how a college presents its offerings in world affairs depends upon the interests and talents of the faculty and

[39] *Princeton Alumni Weekly,* LIII (March 20, 1953), 10–19, and *Official Register of Princeton University: The Undergraduate Catalogue Issue for 1956–1957,* pp. 339–40.

students, the history and location of the institution, internal politics, or administrative planning or accident. All these factors have played some part in developing majors in world affairs for American colleges.

Separate departments of international relations are rare in undergraduate colleges. They exist at only a handful of institutions —among them, American University, Bradley University, the University of Denver, Georgetown University, Lehigh University, San Francisco State College, the University of Southern California, the Woodrow Wilson Department of Foreign Affairs at the University of Virginia, and the Woodrow Wilson School of Public and International Affairs at Princeton University. In most instances, special circumstances have operated to bring the separate departments or schools into being.

As their names imply, the department at Virginia and the school at Princeton owe much to the inspiration of Woodrow Wilson, who had very close ties to both institutions. Wilson's battle to get the United States to join the League of Nations put him at the head of those who believed that the United States had important responsibilities in the modern world. His vision inspired many who came after him, and both Princeton and the University of Virginia acknowledge the inspiration.

Wilson himself had no connection with either American or Georgetown University, but the conduct of World War I, the senatorial debate over the Treaty of Versailles, and the presence of Wilson in the capital as President of the United States, focused world attention on Washington as a center of world affairs. With foreign diplomats and embassies from all the nations in the world located there, Washington is a natural place to study world affairs. Georgetown legitimately regards itself as "one of the pioneers in placing the foreign service profession on a scientific basis, and in developing a curriculum in consular and diplomatic work and for foreign trade."[40]

[40] *Georgetown University, General Information Bulletin* (1955), p. 45.

The Department of International Relations at Lehigh, established in 1947, the School of International Service at American University, which opened in 1958, and the Institute of International Studies at Bradley University originated as responses to the increasing importance in the postwar world of the United States' role in world affairs.

In the West, the inspiration is primarily that of public-spirited citizens with an interest in world affairs. At the University of Denver, it was James H. Causey, a trustee of the university, who founded the Social Science Foundation in that city in 1923 as "The Foundation for the Advancement of the Social Sciences of the University of Denver." And the foundation has always had a great interest in international relations.

In the case of the School of International Relations of the University of Southern California, the chief motivating force came from the university's chancellor, Rufus Bernhard von Kleinsmid, whose interest in international affairs led him, as university president in 1924, to establish a world affairs curriculum leading to a university degree. The School of International Relations has developed from this curriculum. It was formerly a separately organized and independently administered affiliate of the university but is now an integral part of the institution, administered through the College of Letters, Arts, and Sciences. In addition, its faculty serves as the international relations faculty of the Division of Social Studies in the university.[41]

The early concern of San Francisco State College with international relations was inspired by Olive Thompson Cowell, who first offered a course with that title in 1927. Every semester since then, the college has made available courses in the field to its students. By 1936 it offered fifteen semester units, available as electives or as part of a major in international relations. In 1950, the college established a Department of International Relations,

[41] *Bulletin of the University of Southern California: School of International Relations* (1954), pp. 7–10, and *Bulletin of the University of Southern California: College of Letters, Arts, and Sciences* (1957–58), pp. 173–76.

one of six (the other five are anthropology, economics, government, history, and sociology) within a Social Science Division. The special historical circumstances which brought these separate departments and schools into existence did not, of course, guarantee that they would assume a common form within their universities. Thus, the Woodrow Wilson Department of Foreign Affairs at the University of Virginia, up to 1952, was known as a School and awarded the degree of Bachelor of Arts in Foreign Affairs. After 1952, the university no longer awarded this degree, but required undergraduates majoring in foreign affairs to fulfill all the requirements of the College of Arts and Sciences for the bachelor of arts degree. Originally, the department was separately organized and administered under a full-time director and it had its own faculty, but it exists now on the same footing as other university departments.[42]

At Princeton, the Woodrow Wilson School of Public and International Affairs is a cooperative activity of the Departments of Politics, History, and Economics and Sociology, and its faculty members are professors in the several cooperating departments of the university. The school awards the regularly matriculated Princeton undergraduates who meet its requirements with distinction a special certificate in addition to their bachelor's diploma.[43]

Georgetown offers a degree of Bachelor of Science in Foreign Service, and its faculty, composed of persons with considerable practical experience, public or private, in the various fields of international relations and business administration is distinct from the undergraduate College of Arts and Sciences.[44]

At the University of Denver, the Social Science Foundation

[42] "The University of Virginia and World Affairs," *Universities and World Affairs,* Document No. 79 (Mimeographed; New York: Carnegie Endowment for International Peace, 1955), p. 2.

[43] *Official Register of Princeton University: The Undergraduate Catalogue Issue for 1956–1957,* p. 339.

[44] *Georgetown University, Catalogue of the School of Foreign Service* (1956), pp. 30–34.

staff serves as the Department of International Relations in the university. It carries into effect the recommendations of a Committee of Seven of the university (charged with developing a curriculum in the area of international studies), and is conducted by professors representing the social science and modern language departments.[45]

The programs offered in international affairs at all these colleges are interdisciplinary. At Princeton, for example, the work is organized to include eight one-term courses selected from the Departments of History, Politics, and Economics and Sociology, or is arranged on a regional basis (Latin America, the Near East, or the Far East) with the cooperation of the Departments of Germanic and Romance Languages and Literatures and the Department of Oriental Studies. The student may thus enroll in a program emphasizing the history, social institutions, and culture of one region.

At the University of Virginia, the students select thirty hours of work (ten one-term courses), eighteen of them in the Department of Foreign Affairs, and twelve in related departments, of which six are in history, political science, geography, or cultural anthropology, and six are in international economics.

At Denver, students take sixty quarter hours of course work in international studies and related fields .The Denver faculty helps the students fashion programs designed to meet their individual needs and desires from a wide range of courses in anthropology, economics, English, geography, history, humanities, philosophy, political science, psychology, religion, social science, and sociology.

At the University of Southern California, students may pursue one of two majors in international relations through the School of International Relations, stressing either politics or economics. Both groups of students are required to complete in the lower

[45] The University of Denver, *The Program of Studies in International Affairs* (Denver: Social Science Foundation, n.d.), p. 7.

division four semesters in a foreign language and a one-year Introduction to International Relations. Students stressing politics include among their prerequisites a one-semester course in the Fundamentals of Economics; those stressing economics, a two-semester course in Principles of Economics. The students primarily interested in international politics then take three two-semester courses in the Fundamentals of International Politics, American Diplomacy, and International Law, a one-semester course in Principles of International Trade and Exchange, one six-unit elective in regional diplomatic history and relations, and a three-point elective in the Departments of both Political Science and Economics. Students primarily interested in international economics include in their upper-division programs work in the conduct of foreign policy and international organization instead of diplomacy and law, and must take five semester-courses in economics instead of one. The university also offers a "divisional major" in international relations, which includes eighteen upper-division units in international relations and twelve in other social sciences.

Students at Georgetown College of Arts and Sciences who take some of their major work in the School of Foreign Service, must take twenty-four hours of course work in the Department of Government, eighteen of them in international relations and six in a second field of government (political theory and comparative government, American government, or public administration). The college requires students to take twelve hours of history, and the department encourages its majors to take related courses in economics and history. At Lehigh University, the students also take twenty-four hours of work in a program which stresses diplomacy; international organization, law, and theory; and history and government.

The plans at American University envisage an offering which allows students considerable flexibility. All the programs build on a liberal arts base, conceived especially to help students understand their own civilization and another culture, master a foreign language, and develop a satisfying personal philosophy. To these ends the university requires students in the School of International Service to take two two-year courses in American Civilization and Human Behavior and to learn to speak and read one modern language in addition to their native tongue. Students must also register for an honors section in English Composition which allows them to read and write on questions of value, ethics, and religion. Other courses required are Basic Geography, Science and Mathematics, Backgrounds of Civilization, World Politics, and a course in philosophy.

The School of International Service offers six programs to its students, five of them oriented toward specific careers. For those with a general interest in world affairs or primarily interested in teaching, research, or journalism, the school offers an academic major in International Relations and Organization requiring twenty-four hours of work. The student makes up his program by taking nine hours in one of the following fields: international organization and administration, international law and legislation, international political relations, American diplomacy, and the United Nations; and at least three hours each in three of the others. In addition he takes work in economics, geography, history, political science, psychology, and language or statistics.

Alternatively, the student of International Relations and Organization may offer for a major, work in an area (Eastern Europe, Latin America, Southeastern Asia, the Far East, and Africa south of the Sahara), taking an introductory course and electing one full-year seminar (twenty-four credit-hours) in the area he chooses. Each seminar treats the geography, demography, and ecology of the region; its social structure and historical roots; and its religion, culture, economy, government and domestic politics, and its contemporary international politics; it also allows students to study particular countries within the area. Supporting courses (fifteen hours) in languages or social sciences are also required.

The School of International Service also cooperates with the School of Government and Public Administration in offering a combined major in political science in the College of Arts and Science, where students complete a minimum of thirty-six hours in the fields of government and public administration and international relations and organization, with at least twelve hours in each field, in addition to fifteen hours of courses in the social sciences, of which twelve must be beyond the introductory level.

The five career programs which the School of International Service offers are in Foreign Service, International Administration, Overseas Representation, Church Missions, and Overseas Business. The program in Foreign Service requires students to include in their first two years six hours of economics (including a special section in international economics) and one course in the general field of international law or relations. The junior and senior years' work is largely built around two series of seminars and problem papers or "laboratory" courses. The seminars, which meet for extended periods two or three times a week, allow students to investigate closely some broad aspect of international affairs. The students must take four seminars: one primarily historical, one primarily economic, one primarily in the field of contemporary international relations and organization, and a fourth of his own choice.

The school plans to offer seminars in American diplomatic history, underdeveloped areas, international economic problems, the role of the military in foreign affairs, the formulation of foreign policy, early patterns in modern international law and organization, political and economic concepts of peoples and states, selected area problems in international relations, and international administration. In the required six hours of work on problem papers or laboratory work—the school offers six more hours as electives—the student prepares reports, "position papers," and drafts of speeches. He makes up the balance of his program from a specified list of related courses.

The program in International Administration, offered in co-operation with the School of Government and Public Administration, stresses, more than the other programs, courses in public administration and international organization, and the School of International Service strongly recommends, and helps students to arrange, a summer internship in an international agency. The school expects its students in the Overseas Representation program to spend one summer abroad in a controlled cross-cultural program such as the Experiment in International Living, in a Methodist or American Friends Service Committee work camp, or an approved summer session at a foreign university. The program requirements in international administration are quantitatively more than for any of the other programs—an extra summer or even a fifth year may be necessary—because students must master French and one other foreign language peculiar to the area of their major interest.

The Church Missions program allows students to concentrate on particular geographical areas; emphasizes relevant courses in religion; and permits students to work out cooperative undertakings in nursing, agriculture, and other technical fields with other institutions. The Business Overseas program, offered in part by the School of Business Administration, stresses economics and business courses and recommends particularly a course in the economics of underdeveloped areas.

At another new school, the Institute of International Studies at Bradley University, students take eight more credit hours than the university usually requires in order to include in their program required work in history (modern European and American), political science (systems and philosophy), economics (theory and practice), sociology (classes and mores), geography (topography and climate), and six semesters of foreign languages. The institute offers programs in Government Foreign Service and International Trade.

The divisional arrangement at San Francisco State College

gives the students considerable flexibility. The international relations major takes thirty-three semester units, including a core (twelve to fifteen units) of international relations courses: introduction to the field of study, international politics, international law, international organization, and a senior seminar. The student takes the balance of his eighteen to twenty-one units in a geographical area (Far East, Middle East and Africa, Western Europe, Eastern Europe and the U.S.S.R., and Latin America) or a combination of the social sciences (geography and economics; history and government; or sociology, anthropology, and psychology).[46]

A number of institutions without the special geographical or historical forces making for separate departments or schools in international affairs but with a desire to offer world affairs to undergraduates have done so by arranging for interdepartmental cooperation of various types, some quite formally organized, others not.

Agnes Scott College is a good example of the simplest organizational arrangements. The college does not actually offer a major in international relations, but a student may, by combining courses in history and political science, concentrate in world affairs, and superior students may supplement course offerings by independent study on international problems.[47]

Informal cooperation between the political science and history departments, quite feasible for a college like Agnes Scott (enrollment about 600), is not, however, the universal pattern even for

[46] *The Study and Teaching of International Relations at San Francisco State College* (Processed; San Francisco: Division of Social Science, San Francisco State College, n.d.). For the other programs described, see *The School of International Service, Catalog Issue 1958–1961* (Washington: American University, January 1958); *The Institute of International Studies* (Peoria, Ill.: Bradley University, n.d.); and *Bradley University Bulletin . . . 1959–1960*, pp. 235–38.

[47] "Agnes Scott College and World Affairs," *University and World Affairs,* Document No. 47 (Mimeographed; New York: Carnegie Endowment for International Peace, 1954), pp. 1–3.

institutions with a small student body. Clark University (enrollment 1,410), for example, administers its undergraduate work in
international relations through a joint committee (created in
1948) from the Economics, Geography, and History Departments.[48] Other colleges employ similar interdepartmental committees, although the specific cooperating departments vary with
the college. In certain institutions which offer undergraduates
the opportunity to study a particular geographical area in some
detail as a major, the range of departments is quite wide. Thus,
at the State University of Iowa, a student may study in the Program of Foreign Studies, cooperatively administered by an interdepartmental committee with representatives from economics,
geography, history, journalism, the various foreign languages,
oriental studies, political science, and sociology and anthropology.[49] In International Studies at Miami University, the faculty
supervises the work of a student in the International Studies Program through the various departments concerned with languages,
literature, economics, government, history, geography, art, sociology and anthropology, and philosophy and religion.[50]

Sometimes students are offered a bill of fare from which they
may choose their own courses without formal departmental su-
pervision, as at the City College of New York, where students may
arrange a major in international relations by selecting from a
list of courses prepared by an Office of Curricular Guidance from

[48] "Clark University and World Affairs," *Universities and World Affairs,*
Document No. 44 (Mimeographed; New York: Carnegie Endowment for International Peace, 1954), pp. 1, 3. Clark University identifies itself with a
tradition in international relations going back to the work of George Hub-
bard Blakeslee, who in 1908 offered one of the earliest courses in international
relations in this country.
[49] "The State University of Iowa and World Affairs," *Universities and
World Affairs,* Document No. 80 (Mimeographed; New York: Carnegie Endowment for International Peace, 1955), pp. 19–20.
[50] "Miami University in World Affairs," *Universities and World Affairs,*
Document No. 40 (Mimeographed; New York: Carnegie Endowment for International Peace, 1954), p. 19, and *Miami University Announcements for
1959–60,* p. 75.

among the offerings in the Departments of Government, Economics, History, Sociology and Anthropology, Geology, and Philosophy.[51]

Those institutions which do not have formal departments of international relations or interdepartmental majors in international affairs may offer a major in international relations within one department. Single departments which offer instruction in international relations do so in various ways. The possibility of majoring in international relations may be mentioned in the college catalogue without specifying courses, the actual program to be arranged by an adviser (as at Washington Square College of Arts and Science of New York University). The department may prepare a list of recommended courses (as at Michigan State University) without requiring any specific courses. Or the college may regard some courses as core courses, reserving to itself the right to adjust the exact content from year to year (as at Sweet Briar College).

Even if they do not provide a major in world affairs, good liberal arts institutions invariably do offer courses which a student of world affairs would ordinarily include in his own program. And the courses required for a degree will undoubtedly contain material bearing on world affairs. A student in such a college can always arrange his own major by choosing his elective courses judiciously.

At a college like Bowdoin, for instance, there is no major in international relations. On the other hand, the student will study international trade for two weeks if he chooses a course on Principles of Economics, get the historical background on current problems like German unification and touch on developing international organizations in the twentieth century in a history survey course, study American diplomatic history and contem-

[51] "The City College and World Affairs," *Universities and World Affairs,* Document No. 58 (Mimeographed; New York: Carnegie Endowment for International Peace, 1954), p. 12.

porary international problems in a course in the History of the United States, and analyze British foreign policy and the evolution of the Commonwealth in the History of England. In his Introduction to Sociology the student studies world population problems and the problems of urban communities throughout the world. History of Religions, where it touches on the role of religion in various cultures, also contains material relating to international relations. The college also offers ten courses (four in history, five in government, and one in economics) primarily concerned with world affairs: International Economic Problems, International Law, International Organization, Problems of World Politics, Comparative Government, History of Europe from 1848–1914, History of Russia and East Central Europe, and Recent European History, the last dealing almost completely with current international problems. Bowdoin College believes that these courses, taken together furnish a good core of instruction for anyone interested in world affairs.[52]

A similar situation can be found at Hiram College, where students take basic courses in economics, political science, history, sociology, and foreign languages. They have available six-hour courses in The Principles and Problems of International Relations, Foreign Governments, Europe Since 1550, and Recent World History and three-hour courses in International Law, History of the Far East, and Latin American History, plus courses on cultural anthropology and world religions and additional instruction in language and literature.[53]

If one compares the possibilities available to students for studying world affairs under these various options, the actual

[52] "Report on Bowdoin College and World Affairs," *Universities and World Affairs,* Document No. 33 (Mimeographed; New York: Carnegie Endowment for International Peace, 1954), pp. 1–3, and the *Bowdoin College Bulletin, 1956–1957.* The courses in Comparative Government and the History of Russia and East Central Europe are each two-semester offerings.

[53] "Hiram College and World Affairs," *Universities and World Affairs,* Document No. 45 (Mimeographed; New York: Carnegie Endowment for International Peace, 1954), p. 1.

course content does not differ greatly. In some institutions informal arrangements are entirely effective; in others, more elaborate administrative plans are necessary. Universities offering graduate instruction in fields also open to undergraduates are obviously going to try to integrate curricular policies for both groups of students. Colleges instructing undergraduates about more than one geographical area will undoubtedly administer their programs differently from colleges offering only one undergraduate area concentration.[54]

Since students with a consuming interest in world affairs may arrange good programs for themselves under many administrative umbrellas, the principal reason for providing a program of study in world affairs and describing it in the college catalogue is to call to the student's attention the opportunity for studying such a selection of courses and keep him from losing himself in the underbrush of the catalogue. The test of effective education in world affairs lies less in how the college or university organizes its offerings formally than in what it does to call the possibilities of majoring in world affairs to students' attention and in the extent to which its rules are flexible enough to permit students to arrange programs in world affairs. A student may quite legitimately develop an interest in world affairs and acquire valuable insights about them by approaching the subject through many disciplines: economics, geography, language, law, politics, psychology, sociology, or others. No one can say decisively at present which approach will ultimately prove most fruitful, so that a college concerned with world affairs is obliged to offer students an interdepartmental program, no matter how administered, which is both flexible and disciplined—flexible enough to ac-

---

[54] The administrative arrangements for Russian studies at California (Berkeley), Fordham, Indiana, Michigan, Washington, and Yale are affected by the graduate programs, and those at California (Berkeley), Michigan, Stanford, Washington, and Yale (and, to a lesser extent, Indiana and Syracuse) are influenced by other undergraduate area programs on other regions. (Discussed by Deming Brown, "A Report . . . ," pp. 4–5.)

commodate the student's primary interest and to meet the wide-ranging demands of the subject itself, and disciplined so as to give him depth of understanding.[55]

In some cases, the potential for a good program exists, but college administrators have failed to capitalize on it. At one university, for instance, where there is no department of international relations, a student primarily interested in international affairs would have to study world affairs through either the Department of History or the Department of Political Science. The History Department of the university requires its majors to take forty-two quarter term hours. Nine of these hours could be taken in a course in American Foreign Relations; nine more in a related field (for example, political science or economics); and with well-chosen electives, the interested student could get a degree in history which was in fact a concentration in international relations. In political science, it would be even easier to concentrate informally in international relations, because the student may include twenty quarter hours in international relations proper, and by judiciously electing courses in history, geography, anthropology, and economics, could develop a considerable and impressive major.

This university's offerings in international relations are very extensive, but the principal drawback for the student who wishes to study world affairs there is the university's failure to point out the possibility. If a student takes the initiative and lets his adviser know of his interest, or if the adviser discovers it and points out to the student that the curriculum is available, the possibilities may be realized. "Experience has shown, however," Deming Brown has noted, "that only rarely do undergraduates possess the single-mindedness and foresight required in planning a four-year course of study which will give them a disciplinary major

55 See, for instance, Hans J. Morgenthau, "Area Studies and the Study of International Relations," *International Social Science Bulletin*, IV (1952), 654; and Grayson L. Kirk, "The Study of International Relations in American Universities," *Southern University Conference Proceedings 1947*, p. 56; and Kirk, *The Study of International Relations in American Colleges and Universities*, p. 55.

and, simultaneously a well-rounded background" merely by majoring in one discipline and by devising his own program of studies in world affairs.[56] It is not the course offerings but the lack of guidance which is critical here. When the matter was analyzed in 1954, the university survey team pointed out that the university could appoint an additional adviser for the social studies programs with a special interest in international relations, that the university catalogue could inform students clearly about the possibility of arranging to concentrate in international relations, and that the university could set up an interdepartmental international relations planning committee to suggest patterns of study for students wishing to concentrate in international relations. None of these steps has been taken, however, at this writing although presumably there is no obstacle to taking such steps in the future.

The Universities and World Affairs survey and the series of Studies in Universities and World Affairs (of which the present volume is a part) clearly show that the lack of consensus about what belongs under the rubic "world affairs" runs parallel to a lack of consensus about the best way to present world affairs in the college curriculum. Obviously there is merit in a great variety of programs and in different methods of organizing them; no one set of specific courses or type of formal organization is necessary to permit students to study world affairs. Colleges can provide good programs administered by an adviser, a department, several departments, committees, or schools; the cooperating departments may number three or thirteen; and still a student may study world affairs. The real differences among college programs, now and always, will be in the quality of the teachers,[57] and in their ability to help the student synthesize the materials he studies from the common angle of world affairs referred to in chapter 1.

[56] P. 24. Mr. Brown was writing about Russian area studies but his observation applies as well to all teaching in world affairs.

[57] See Edith Ware, *The Study of International Relations in the United States, Survey for 1938* (New York: Columbia University Press, 1938), p. 123, for an early expression of this point of view.

# CHAPTER EIGHT

# Supplementary Programs and World Affairs

Travel, in the younger sort, is a part of education.
FRANCIS BACON, "Of Travel"

No LIBERAL ARTS FACULTY deludes itself by believing that it can in four years on campus provide its bachelor's degree candidates with the magic formula for living a full life and understanding the world they live in. A college receives students of various abilities, develops their skills and knowledge to the extent that time allows, and sends them on, hoping that they have acquired the abilities and attitudes they will need to continue growing in later years. A college education and life's experiences reinforce each other. Thus, in World War II college graduates were generally deemed better qualified to assume responsibility in the Armed Forces than those without college training, and the World War II veterans displayed in college a maturity, experience, and perspective that made them better students than their younger civilian counterparts.

Teachers have long recognized this reciprocal relationship between life and experience, and colleges have not hesitated to enroll students who were working part time to pay their way. In fact, colleges are more and more requiring students who hold scholarships to help defray part of the cost of their education by taking outside employment. Some American colleges, like Antioch and Bennington, have even formally recognized the mutual value of education and experience by requiring students to spend a specified amount of time off campus on jobs.

Insight into world affairs certainly need not come only from the classroom and library. The traveler who has seen wartime devastation in Europe or Asia, primitive agricultural methods in Spain or India, or the widely varied standards of living between rich and poor in Latin America, understands some essential statistics and geography in a way that even pictures in the books he reads cannot duplicate. Travel alone is not, of course, always educational. The apocryphal story of an American on a commercial guided tour who had to be reminded that "Austria was the country where the innkeeper had a feather in his cap" certainly could have gained from his experience few impressions of any value. But off-campus travel and work have provided mature, carefully selected students with insights and understanding which complement most significantly the liberal arts curriculum.

The most familiar pattern of study overseas is the Junior Year Abroad programs, sponsored by various colleges, and open also to eligible students from other institutions. Among the colleges administering Junior Year Abroad programs are Fordham University (Belgium, France, and Italy); Hamilton College (a program in France); Rosary College (Switzerland); Smith College (France, Italy, Spain, and Switzerland); Sweet Briar College (France); Washington Square College, New York University (Brazil and Spain); and the College of Liberal Arts of Wayne University (Germany).

The Junior Year Abroad programs vary in detail, but in general, the colleges provide students enrolling with preliminary orientation sessions both in the United States and abroad;[1] opportunities for them to study in foreign universities with students of the host countries; the chance to live with a local family;

---

[1] For an interesting survey showing how badly equipped American students are, in general, to profit from their experiences abroad, see *American Students Abroad: Goodwill Ambassadors* (Syracuse, N. Y.: Maxwell Graduate School of Citizenship and Public Affairs, Syracuse University, 1958).

and special courses, programs, and trips. The sponsoring colleges assist students to obtain credit for their work by providing the supplementary American educational apparatus of course examinations and grades.

A typical program is offered by Sweet Briar College. The program begins each year in early September at Tours, France, with a six-week period of intensive language study under native tutors, because before being accepted, each student agrees to use the French language exclusively throughout the period abroad. Toward the end of October the students move to Paris where, for eight months, they may take courses in French language and literature, art, government, history, international affairs, music, philosophy, or political science at many of the leading institutions of higher learning. In addition, students may arrange to take lessons in various studios of painting and sculpture and special courses in subjects like the history of drama, dramatic diction, and dramatic criticism. If the student successfully completes his year's work, he receives thirty hours of credit from his own college. Several scholarships, in varying amounts, are awarded to students with excellent academic records who demonstrate financial need.

Both in Tours and Paris, all students of the group lodge with French families, and thus have the best possible opportunity to hear and speak French and learn about French life, customs, and outlook. A series of extracurricular activities includes visits to museums and monuments and trips to points of historical and artistic interest near Tours and Paris. Social events bring members of the group into touch with French students and with outstanding French personalities.

In recent years, about eighty students have composed an average group, and they normally represent about thirty different colleges and universities. From 1948 to the present, a total of eighty-five colleges and universities have been represented.

Since most colleges and universities quite reasonably prefer to have their seniors in residence, the Year Abroad programs are designed principally for juniors, who have proved to be a mature enough group to benefit from the experience. The programs have, incidentally, often stimulated students to do graduate work both at home and abroad.

One variation of the Junior Year Abroad is offered by Mexico City College. This college, operating along the lines of a liberal arts college in the United States, makes it possible for students to spend a year in Mexico and still pursue their course work in the English language. The college also offers a winter quarter in Mexico for transient students from the United States whose colleges operate on the quarter system. Other universities encourage their students to study abroad during the summer; some have arranged summer courses at foreign universities. The German Department of the University of Washington, for example, offers a summer program at the University of Munich. And Sarah Lawrence College runs its own summer school in Florence, Italy, where students may earn four points of credit toward their degree.[2]

Western College for Women, which allows its students either to participate in the Junior Year Abroad programs of Sweet Briar or Smith Colleges or to arrange independently to study abroad during the junior year, sponsors its own summer travel seminar to a geographic area which students have studied during the school year. Each year the college emphasizes a different area in its Intercultural Studies program (Europe and Africa, 1957–58; Latin America, 1958–59; Middle East, 1959–60; and the Far East, 1960–61), and the summer seminar students visit the area in the following summer. Faculty members conduct the seminar, and although it is open to all qualified students (from Western and other colleges) the college prefers that only those who have com-

[2] Information about programs offering opportunities to study abroad is available from the sponsoring colleges and the International Institute of Education in New York.

pleted their junior year go and use their summer observations in some special study when they return to the campus for the final year.[3] Both the value of the seminars and the way they relate to the program of Intercultural Studies are summed up by one student's remark that she "learned more during . . . five weeks [in the Orient] than . . . during a whole year of study," but that she "wouldn't . . . have gotten half so much out of the seminar if I hadn't studied the Orient before going."[4]

Keuka College has established a most unusual overseas summer program for its students. The college has as a regular part of its degree program a "Field Period," during which it helps junior and senior students get jobs related to their college and professional careers. The Field Period permits the girls to obtain some supervised work experience and acquire a community and world outlook. They prepare, even as freshmen and sophomores, for the field work of their two upper-class years: in the freshman year they have an independent reading period supervised by the English Department, and in the sophomore year, they do volunteer work in an established community agency. Although the college places most of its students in the United States for the Field Period, a number of them may work in foreign countries in the World Emphasis part of the program. The college has actually arranged for students to work in a number of social service agencies (refugee children's camps, neighborhood houses, and hospitals, among others) in Austria, Canada, Finland, France, Germany, Norway, Switzerland, and the United Kingdom.[5] The opportunity not only to live but to work in a foreign country while still a college student is a unique and valuable one.

Combined work-and-study programs, long an integral part of the Antioch College curriculum in the United States, were ex-

3 *Western College Bulletin, 1957–1958*, pp. 38, 39, 70–73.

4 See Dixie Dean Harris, "Asia Serves as a Classroom," *New York Herald Tribune*, Oct. 6, 1957, sec. 2, p. 3.

5 *Keuka's Field Period* (Keuka Park, N. Y.: Keuka College, 1957), pp. 3, 22–23.

tended by the college in 1958 to include work and study abroad. Antioch Education Abroad now operates for a twelve-week fall, winter, or spring term in Mexico and for a full year in nine other countries (Austria, Denmark, Finland, France, Germany, Great Britain, Norway, Sweden, and Switzerland). The college can also make individual arrangements for its students to study and work in Egypt, Italy, and the Netherlands and hopes ultimately to expand their opportunities to study and work anywhere in the world where suitable facilities exist.

Offerings naturally vary from country to country, but they all incorporate the successful features of the traditional Junior Year Abroad programs: field trips, special language training (where needed), special seminars, and residence with foreign families. The college plans the programs individually, placing students according to their ability, in institutions of higher learning as different as the Scandinavian Folk Schools and the highly specialized Austrian and German universities. Only the college's better students are eligible to participate, and the college evaluates their work either by having them prepare reports, asking instructors abroad to submit grades, or by setting special examinations. The college also provides resident directors in Mexico and Europe to keep in touch with the students.

Work periods abroad are the most distinguishing hallmark of Antioch Education Abroad, and, together with the cooperating European institutions, Antioch has arranged for its students abroad to hold jobs in these periods with families and in factories, schools, clinics, hospitals, social service missions, industry, and business. Costs vary, but the college helps the students keep their basic expenses down to amounts comparable to (and, in some cases, less than) costs on the Antioch campus.[6]

Stanford University has announced an interesting variation of

[6] *Antioch College Bulletin,* LIV (March 1958). For the philosophy behind the program, see Samuel B. Gould, "The University's Stake in Educational Travel," in *The American Student Abroad 1956–1957* (New York: Council on Student Travel [1958]), pp. 5–7.

the study-abroad plans. It has established a study center near Stuttgart with dormitories and classrooms where, beginning in June 1958, groups of sixty regularly enrolled sophomores and juniors have been able to study for six months. Two Stanford faculty couples are in residence, and courses will, for the most part, fit into Stanford's general studies program, emphasizing European literature, history, culture, and economics. Native teachers provide intensive language courses, and the university offers students academic credit for the work they undertake.

Colgate University has opened a temporary southern branch of their college at Mendoza, Argentina, where honors students spend one semester studying with Argentine professors. The students attend separate classes, but they live with families in the city and associate with the students at the National University of Cuyo. The program is partly subsidized by the Williams Foundation and may continue indefinitely if it proves successful.

Lake Erie College has even gone so far as to require all juniors as part of the B.A. curriculum to spend their winter quarter abroad in either Denmark, France, Germany, Holland, Italy, or Switzerland. Another college may even require its B.A. candidates to study abroad for a full year.[7]

Student enthusiasm for such projects as these is evident not only from their continuing participation but from the efforts they themselves have made on several campuses to create special programs of student travel and study with academic standing. Students at the University of Minnesota, for instance, developed the Student Project for Amity among Nations (SPAN) just after World War II. Managed by students and faculty members, SPAN selects from the colleges of Minnesota several teams of eight or ten students to make trips abroad each summer with a faculty adviser. The students prepare for their trips by studying for a

---

[7] Harlan Cleveland, "The Real International World and Academic Lag," in Roy A. Price (ed.), *New Viewpoints in the Social Sciences* (Washington: National Council for the Social Studies, 1958), p. 188, and correspondence with Dean Cleveland.

full year the language, history, and contemporary problems of the country they will visit. They also begin research for a paper they will complete and submit for credit to their own college authorities after they return. SPAN raises its own funds throughout the state, former participants contribute their services to carry on the administrative work of the organization and help organize subsequent trips.

Similar student fund-raising efforts at the University of California at Berkeley and Los Angeles have brought into being Project PIC (Pakistan, India, and Ceylon) and Project India to promote student travel to these countries and to help students from Asia who are attending the university.[8]

Students have also expressed their interest and concern in world affairs through their extracurricular programs, which often relate so closely to curricular efforts in the international field that they deserve full support of faculties and administrations. The leading student organization in these matters is the National Student Association. The association has since 1948 been a leading agency in the field of student travel, and it has arranged some of its summer tours to permit American students to visit with important personages abroad in the arts, sciences, and government. The association, through its International Relations Commission, has also undertaken to improve extracurricular programs in world affairs on campus, helping colleges to take advantage of the people and facilities now available to nearly every American institution of higher learning: these include foreign students on campus; visiting lecturers from foreign countries; forums sponsored by student, faculty, and service organizations; and the activities of local Collegiate Councils for the United Nations, International Relations Clubs, and their national counterparts.[9]

[8] See Howard E. Wilson, *American College Life as Education in World Outlook* (Washington: American Council on Education, 1956), pp. 149–59, for further details about these and similar projects.

[9] *Ibid., passim.*

Still another important contribution to an understanding of world affairs is made by those colleges offering fellowships to deserving graduates for a year of study abroad after they receive their B.A. degrees. Columbia College, for instance, has available the Henry Evans Traveling Fellowship ($1,000) for graduates "who have shown ability of high order and whose interest in the world about them is such as to give promise of well rounded development"; Harvard College makes awards from the Frederick Shelden Fund for Travelling Fellowships to further the education of "students of promise and standing in the University by providing them with facilities for further education by travel after graduation. . . . "; and the Woodrow Wilson School of Public and International Affairs at Princeton has given scholarships to students for summer study abroad to help them do research for their senior theses. Here again is a type of opportunity of unlimited merit which should commend itself both to private and public philanthropy.

Although travel and study abroad are sometimes—but not, for instance, at Stanford or Antioch—a more expensive education than that on campus, the impact of the experience on properly prepared students is something the instructor in the classroom can only aspire to. As part of training in world affairs it is invaluable, and it is unfortunate that the opportunity is not more widely available.

The Junior Year Abroad and other programs described above are well conceived and executed. They deserve to be copied and expanded. One of the principal difficulties in expanding them is financial, of course, but one may hope that, in a world-minded nation, they may command the support of foundations and industries.[10]

[10] The Mobil Overseas Oil Company gave summer jobs abroad to eight juniors and two graduate students, hoping to interest them in permanent positions with the company after graduation. To acquaint them with local customs, the company arranged for students to live with families abroad in France, Italy, Germany, Mexico, Nigeria, and the United Kingdom. See "10 Students Venture Forth . . . " *New York Times*, June 28, 1957, p. 31.

CHAPTER NINE

# Conclusions

If today will not, tomorrow may.

THOMAS FULLER, *Gnomologia*, No. 2725

TODAY, AS IN THE PAST, prescribing a curriculum leading to the B.A. degree is a delicate matter, requiring us to understand not only the needs of the moment but the fundamental requirements of civilization. To meet effectively the challenges posed by the Soviet sputnik, for instance, colleges know that they cannot merely intensify their instruction in science and mathematics. They must also open man's eyes to the great drama being acted out on the stage of the world—and the universe. Man's conquest of space will, to be sure, be a technical and scientific victory, but it also heralds a new age with implications, now only vaguely sensed, for philosophy, the arts, literature, and politics. In the words of one prominent scientist,[1] "The poetically beautiful patterns of modern scientific knowledge bear fresh witness in a whole new range of thoughts and qualities and dimensions to the Psalmist's ancient cry: 'The heavens declare the glory of God and the firmament showeth His handiwork.' " Students being trained in our colleges today must be able to cope in more than scientific terms with this new era and its new concepts. They must know that although survival for Americans depends in part on the insights and technical skills of the nation's scientists, it de-

[1] Dr. Merle A. Tuve of the Carnegie Institution, quoted in *New York Times,* March 24, 1958, p. 19.

165

pends as well on the ability of statesmen and ordinary citizens to cope with the problems of world affairs.

The primary obligation that college faculties have in improving education in world affairs is to determine whether the traditional approaches to the subject, adequate and useful as they were in their own time, still meet the needs of our undergraduates. Just as scholars at the turn of the century had to make room for colleagues seeking to understand and interpret world politics in terms larger than those of law and history, so must scholars today allow for teaching and research in world affairs in terms larger still. They must somehow bring together these arts and sciences whose combined insights alone can resolve the dilemmas of the modern world.

Because ecology is as important in administering a college or university as in understanding biology,[2] educational institutions must continue to seek out their own ways of studying and teaching about world affairs. Although no one set of blueprints can satisfy everyone completely, the most successful designs to date are those which incorporate interdisciplinary patterns. These patterns are not necessarily elaborate. Special schools or departments often provide excellent instruction in world affairs for undergraduates, but useful as such arrangements are, they are clearly essential only for the largest universities. On the other hand, because every discipline and phase of college and university life is actually involved when these institutions adjust themselves to international realities, providing adequate programs in world affairs is in truth a problem for an entire faculty and administration; it cannot be left to one department alone.[3] Colleges most concerned with world affairs do not regard departmental lines as divinely prescribed; they always recognize them for what

[2] See John M. Gaus, "The Ecology of Government," *Reflections on Public Administration* (University, Ala.: University of Alabama Press, 1957), pp. 1–19.

[3] See Howard E. Wilson, *Universities and World Affairs* (New York: Carnegie Endowment for International Peace, 1951), pp. 36–37, 71–72.

they are—administrative devices created to advance teaching and research. They realize that although closeting students of world affairs within one department will not make their work wholly sterile—the best students at least will always find ways of viewing the broad horizons—it may nevertheless deprive them of some of the seminal influences inherent in the liberal arts.

To learn about world affairs, students need an atmosphere where they can begin to see the wholeness of knowledge; where they learn how to enrich their lives through the humane, social, and natural studies; where they can take courses that relate the areas of knowledge to one another, not just in a nostalgic attempt to recapture an unattainable medieval unity, but rather to make the liberal arts as meaningful as possible; and where they understand that even if it is impossible today to take all knowledge to be their province, they can still derive something significant from the entire range of liberal arts and sciences.

Effective teaching in world affairs occurs where the curriculum and the faculty spirit are truly liberal; where faculty members teach students and not just subject matter; where they try to develop minds and not merely drill automatons; where world affairs permeates the curriculum and appears to some extent in all required courses; and where the college deliberately helps the student relate all his studies to world affairs. In short, if a college or university regards itself as veritably a community of scholars, it can undoubtedly create an effective undergraduate program in world affairs.

Such a program can be an important asset to a liberal arts college, useful not only to future specialists but to students whose professional concerns will ultimately remove them from frequent or direct contact with world affairs. For the student who plans to be a professional in world affairs—to do graduate work and then teach or work for the United States government, an international organization, or an industry with branches overseas—the broad, interdisciplinary program introduces him to his subject and prepares him to work in one or more disciplines in graduate school. The broader his background is, the more effective he will be; and if he can bring together a meaningful group of courses in economics, history, politics, psychology, philosophy, and sociology; elect additional courses in art, literature, and music; and study foreign languages throughout his college career, he will be ably equipped for the future.[4]

But the world affairs program should also be open to tomorrow's architects, businessmen, dentists, engineers, lawyers, physicians, scientists, and other professional men, who will be better and happier in their professions if their specialized graduate training rests on a sound liberal arts base. No college can afford to allow its students to ignore the technical prerequisites of their professional studies, but it should also encourage them to acquire as broad a background as possible, to use the unique facilities of the liberal arts college to study outside their professional fields, before they undertake their professional training.[5] There is no reason, for instance, why future physicians should not major in music or world affairs; engineers, in literature or art; and businessmen, in history or languages. There will be ample time for them to indulge their specialties after college, but never again such excellent opportunities to learn about other fields. And the well-conceived world affairs program in a liberal arts college is admirably suited to give many students the knowledge and understanding they need for rich and full lives.

Though faculties cannot by themselves handle all the obstacles between them and an ideal world affairs program, there are some steps they can take at once toward this objective. They can, for instance, provide courses giving students the opportunity to analyze international problems. Each faculty must determine in

[4] See C. Dale Fuller, *Training of Specialists in International Relations* (Washington: American Council on Education, 1957), p. 124.

[5] See, for example, statements by the deans of the graduate schools, Harvard University, *Comments on Pre-Professional Training* (Cambridge, Mass.: Prepared for the Board of Freshman Advisers, 1949).

the light of its own curriculum how best its students may examine the issues they need to understand as citizens, but some required course in world affairs is an indispensable part of liberal education in the twentieth century. The conventional introductory course in international relations, offered as it is now primarily with the needs of future majors in mind, is not, however, the most appropriate course for colleges to require. A course in problems of world affairs or more specifically in problems of United States foreign policy would, on the other hand, be invaluable. Here financial support of foundations to make available case studies or problem materials could greatly enhance the value of the courses.

To teach about world affairs adequately today, however, the liberal arts colleges must learn how to correct a fault arising out of their greatest virtue. As products of Western civilization, our colleges are steeped in Western cultural traditions, which they cherish and strengthen. But what is best in Western cultural traditions can survive only if Westerners understand the values, hopes, and ambitions of non-Western peoples and help them use constructively the revolutionary forces inspired by, but too often directed against, the West. Western universities must devise truly global curricula. Teachers and students must recognize how important it is to learn more about the great cultures outside the Western world. Courses in anthropology and in non-Western languages, literatures, history, and philosophies are no longer luxuries—they are necessities.[6]

[6] See Vera Micheles Dean, *The American Student and the Non-Western World* (Cambridge, Mass.: Harvard University Press, 1956), p. 24. See also William G. Carleton, "Wanted: Wiser Teachers of International Relations," *Journal of Higher Education,* XXV (1954), 4–5; Harlan Cleveland, "The Real International World and the Academic Lag," in Roy A. Price (ed.), *New Viewpoints in the Social Sciences* (Washington: National Council for the Social Studies, 1958), pp. 172–88; *Final Report of the Southeastern Assembly on the United States and Far East* (Atlanta, Ga.: Emory University, 1958); S. B. Gould, "Education's Mount Everest," *Antioch Notes,* XXXII (May 15, 1955), [3–4]; Howard Mumford Jones, "Education and One World," in Lyman Bryson, Louis Finkelstein, and R. M. MacIver (eds.), *Goals for American*

Developing non-Western studies requires considerable planning, money, and labor, but the successful attempts to provide such programs should encourage others. At the University of Arizona, for instance, bringing together the resources of the university, establishing an interdepartmental Committee on Oriental Studies, and appointing a specialist in Asian Studies, has helped create a Program of Oriental Studies today where none existed before 1956. Columbia College, by careful work since 1945 has, with the help of the Carnegie Corporation, developed courses in Oriental Humanities and the History and Culture of the Orient, and has also made available a three-volume *Introduction to Oriental Civilizations* (one volume each on Japan, India, and China), which is a boon to instructors throughout the country.[7] It is even possible, once these reading materials are more accessible, that the Columbia faculty may seriously consider allowing undergraduates to choose between the Western and Oriental civilization courses to fulfill their basic require-

---

*Education* (New York: Harper & Bros., 1950), p. 228; Hyman Kublin, *An Introductory Reading Guide to Asia* (New York: Asia Society, 1958); Cornelis de Kiewiet, "Let's Globalize Our Universities," *Saturday Review of Literature,* Sept. 12, 1953, pp. 13 ff.; Ward Morehouse, *Educational and Cultural Activity in Asia: An Account of Recent Developments in the United States* (New York: Asia Society, 1958); F. S. C. Northrop, "Education for Intercultural Understanding," *Journal of Higher Education,* XVIII (1947), 177–81; Harold E. Snyder, "What Are Some of the More Effective Ways of Reshaping Programs of General Education To Equip Students More Adequately To Cope with America's Changing Role in International Relations?" *Current Issues in Higher Education* (1955), pp. 312–13; William G. Tyrrell, "Developing International Understanding in the First Two Years of College," in Howard R. Anderson (ed.), *Approaches to an Understanding of World Affairs* (Washington: National Council for the Social Studies, 1954), pp. 383–95; Francis O. Wilcox, "Foreign Policy and Some Implications for Education," U.S. Department of State, *Bulletin,* XXXVII (1957), 179–80, and "Education for Overseasmanship," *NEA Journal,* XLVI (1957), 505.

[7] For a fuller account of these and other programs, see Asia Society, "Asian Studies in Undergraduate Education" (Mimeographed; New York: The Society, 1957); and Ward Morehouse, *Educational and Cultural Activity in Asia.* See also Eugene P. Boardman, *Asian Studies in Liberal Education* (Washington: Association of American Colleges, 1959), and Hugh Borton, "Asian Studies and the American College," *Journal of Asian Studies,* XVIII (November 1958), 59–65.

ments. Another interesting group of courses is made available by those administering the degree of bachelor of arts with concentration in the social sciences at the University of Chicago, where students may choose from courses on the development of a non-Western civilization, either Chinese, Islamic, or Indian.[8] Both Chicago and Columbia, with the help of the Carnegie Corporation, have established programs of teaching internships in Asian studies, which provide opportunities for younger specialists to teach non-Western civilization courses and carry on research. Columbia is also carrying on conferences on the problems and means of introducing these subjects into the college curriculum.[9] A few years ago, the University of Rochester decided to give its students the background they needed to identify important issues in the non-Western world and make wise decisions on them. Convinced that no one discipline could give nonspecialist undergraduates this ability, the university assembled a team of experts to provide the instruction.[10] In 1958–59, still another promising development began, with Ford Foundation help, with a fellowship program in East Asian Studies at Harvard University, designed to help liberal arts teachers prepare themselves to teach courses about non-Western peoples.

Besides teaching more about the non-Western world, faculties concerned with world affairs must address themselves to other problems. For instance, language teachers (with the help of social scientists) must find ways of giving their students well-rounded pictures of the societies whose people speak the language they are studying. College faculties in general need to learn how best to evaluate the quantity and quality of education in world affairs in their curricula and how to arrange for faculty members to meet and talk more frequently than they now do about effect-

[8] See Milton Singer (ed.), *Introducing India in Liberal Education* (Chicago: University of Chicago Press, 1957).

[9] Association for Asian Studies, *Newsletter,* IV (November 1958), 3–5.

[10] Warren S. Hunsberger (ed.), *New Era in the Non-Western World* (Ithaca: Cornell University Press, 1957), pp. vii–viii.

ive ways of bringing a global perspective into their courses. Solving these problems will be expensive, and colleges and universities, government agencies, foundations, and industries will have to cooperate to provide the necessary funds.

A good deal of exploration along these lines is already in progress. But successful experiments too often have a limited impact because so few people know about the undertakings and because no one attempts to evaluate the experiments objectively. Professional associations of scholars, with adequate financial support, could undoubtedly establish some central reporting and evaluating agency to keep track of and assess changes in university education in world affairs and inform faculties periodically about them.

Another line of possible progress emerges when one recalls that institutions providing world affairs programs have conceived them either as general or as area programs. The general programs provide the broader survey of world problems; in the area approach the study is geographically confined, but shows the student how wide and deep his understanding must be even to begin to understand world problems. The differences between the two are really in emphasis, and usually students can learn a great deal in either kind of program if it includes some special integrating device such as an honors essay or seminar or individual or small-group instruction.[11] Internships in business and government, student exchange programs, and scholarships to help students finance a junior year abroad or postgraduate study can also strengthen programs of world affairs throughout the country, and more of them are needed.

In introducing or improving a program in world affairs, a college faculty might have to revise some courses and add others to its curriculum. Presumably instructors can always revise their

[11] See Grayson Kirk, *The Study of International Relations in American Colleges and Universities* (New York: Council on Foreign Relations, 1947), pp. 49–51.

courses, but it is by no means easy for a college to add courses to an already overcrowded curriculum. To help students learn the history, languages, and literature they need for a liberal education and a world view, educators might lengthen the college course, but this solution is undesirable for many reasons and primarily because it is unnecessary. Most colleges cannot today offer adequate liberal education in world affairs for the same reason that they cannot offer adequate liberal arts education in any field —because they are not receiving students adequately prepared for college. Many freshmen arrive unable to pursue college-level studies in almost any field of work: they cannot write or speak acceptable English, they do not know a foreign language, they are unequipped to study college mathematics and science, and they do not know much history or geography. The college curriculum inevitably suffers, and although colleges often have to offer remedial work to their degree candidates, they cannot make up in four years what the student has not been taught in twelve.

The weaknesses of liberal arts education in the United States today suddenly became visible to everyone along with the Russian sputnik in 1957, but college teachers have known of the deficiencies for many years. They arise essentially from a philosophical confusion about the meaning of democracy. Contrary to public opinion, the Declaration of Independence, in asserting that "all men are created equal," does not guarantee everyone the innate ability to profit from college. Democracy should guarantee equal educational opportunities, and so long as it does, it may properly refuse to advance students without the interest or capacity for higher education. Democracy can never, unfortunately, guarantee everyone a mind that can benefit from college work. Because education is essentially a matter of quality, schools and colleges must distinguish among students according to their ability if they are to escape the consequences of an educational Gresham's law. State laws requiring high schools to give diplomas to all students who serve their time or requiring colleges to admit every holder of a high school diploma are anti-intellectual. By lowering standards, they defeat the very cause they allegedly espouse—educating the citizenry,[12] and they encourage all those who indulge in the most grotesque educational vices: the administrators who profess that training our youth in school to drive cars is as important as learning to read, the teachers who believe that students in high school should have only one hour of homework a night four times a week (in order to leave Wednesday evening free for viewing television with the family), and the students who prefer courses in Clicking with the Crowd, My Duties as Baby-Sitter, Developing School Spirit, Life Adjustment, and Co-ed Cooking to intellectually rigorous training.

The public secondary school must, without doubt, serve the community which supports it through taxes. High school faculties cannot, as a matter of personal and professional ethics, ignore a community problem affecting their students' lives, whether it be the high death rate among teen-agers in automobile accidents, poor nutrition in the home, juvenile delinquency, or ignorance of personal hygiene. In the best of all possible worlds, other agencies and the students' families would deal with such evils. But when parents and government bureaus ignore these issues or are ineffective in meeting them, the secondary school may be fulfilling a high social responsibility by offering even the much-criticized courses in driving, cooking, life adjustment, or beauty culture.[13] In one sense, these courses could be, as some school administrators have alleged, more important than learn-

[12] As the Educational Policies Commission, National Education Association, reported: "Among high-school graduates qualified to profit from higher education, a tragically large number—in some places as many as half—do not go to college. Lack of money accounts for an important share, but not for all, of this failure. Among the other factors . . . is lack of motivation." *The Contemporary Challenge to American Education* (Washington: The Commission, 1958), p. 11.

[13] See, for instance, Robert Lewis Shayon, "Report from the Grass-Roots," *Saturday Review,* Sept. 13, 1958, p. 16.

ing to read, because they relate to survival, and reading skills may only be a matter of professional advancement.

But while conceding the public function of the secondary school, society should not confuse it with the school's educational responsibilities; the two are complementary, not substitutes for each other. The paramount duty of the secondary school is still to educate its students formally as well as possible, which means that it must challenge them continually. In the ideal public high school, those students who do not plan or are not qualified to go on to liberal arts colleges should receive as good an education as they are capable of absorbing and go on to vocational schools and junior colleges whenever feasible. But students of a liberal arts college caliber need more than they have been receiving as a rule in the average American secondary school: they need to know a body of facts, how to study seriously, what good work habits are, and how to think effectively. Only with improved training along these lines will they come to college properly prepared with training that will not automatically continue to force colleges to lower their standards as they have had to do in the past. It will do us no harm to copy from the Soviet Union the educational priorities that bring them to introduce eight-year-old school children to Chinese, Hindi, and Arabic; to start developing at an early age a group of specialists in the languages, culture, and economics, of the countries concerned; or to use foreign languages as a medium of instruction in history, geography, arithmetic, science, and in extracurricular activities as well. What is more, learning languages at an early age is not something the Soviet Union invented; good English and Continental schools have been doing it for centuries.[14] Even in the United States, a few schools have also offered instruction far above the general average. All the Soviet Union may take credit for is

[14] William F. Aggeler, "The Teaching of English in France," *PMLA*, LXXIII (September 1958), Part 2, 7–14; and P. H. Breitenstein, "The Teaching of Foreign Languages in the Netherlands," *ibid.*, 1–6.

bringing the notion forcefully to American attention. In any case, American schools could profit from the example of all their European counterparts by lengthening the number of hours of foreign language instruction during term time and increasing the number of hours of homework in all subjects.[15]

If our colleges are truly to provide a liberal education, all our schools must emphasize, more than they have in recent years, disciplined instruction for the student bound for college in English, foreign languages, American and European history, science, mathematics, world geography, other cultures, and the humanities. Our colleges must again raise their standards to insist that entering students have the necessary prerequisites for college work. Only after the standards are raised, will there be ample time and opportunity for the college student to undertake advanced language work and to study non-Western history and literatures, which make up the principal gaps in the present college programs. If American college faculties could take for granted in their matriculating students those skills their European counterparts expect as a matter of course, the problem of educating effectively in world affairs will be largely solved.[16]

To take such strides, however, is not at all easy. It means that the American people will have to be willing to spend additional tax monies to construct new schools, train more and better teachers, and pay them better salaries. But the cost is in fact the cost of survival, and it is certainly far cheaper than the cost of the disaster which will ensue if we fail to take these measures.

Re-establishing standards should not, of course, blind us to the admitted virtues of the American educational system or cause us to sacrifice our democratic values. In meeting the challenge which arose in the trail of the Russian sputnik, the American people

15 Potentials for improving secondary school curricula are explored in American Council of Learned Societies, *Newsletter*, IX (1958). See also James B. Conant, *The American High School Today* (New York: McGraw-Hill Book Co., 1959).

16 See, for example, E. L. Woodward, *The Study of International Relations at a University* (Oxford: Clarendon Press, 1948), pp. 20–21.

must be sure not to squander any of the assets in an educational system that helped them master a continent; forge a nation; avoid rigid class barriers; foster "the diversifications of talents, the ingenuity, and the productivity which have brought this society to the highest level of economic prosperity ever known." Moreover, we should certainly continue to provide "the spiritual stamina and fervor for freedom which have preserved individual liberty and guarded equality of opportunity through war and hardship. . . ."[17]

It would also be a mistake to regiment our students, to narrow their opportunities to qualify for higher education, or to emphasize science at the expense of the humanities and the social sciences. And we need not be trapped by any of these pitfalls. If our schools receive the funds they need to create an atmosphere of intellectual drive and to communicate the excitement of education, as the best schools here and abroad already do, they would stimulate students to their greatest possible achievements. More students would aspire to higher goals, and all would be better educated.[18] At the same time, we can recognize the need for differentiated curricula and objectives for students of varying abilities.

We must preserve in our educational system the discipline of free men united in a common cause rather than the discipline imposed from an all-powerful state. We must expand the opportunities for students barred by financial reasons from going on to college. And we must stimulate able students to pursue advanced academic work as far as they can qualify. We must raise our standards, not for scientific studies alone, but for all parts of the curriculum. Higher standards—nothing less—in primary and secondary schools will suffice for a democratic nation with pretensions to lead the world. Today's challenges require science and the arts to march forward hand in hand. Upon further advances

[17] *The Contemporary Challenge to American Education,* p. 7.
[18] See *ibid.,* p. 11.

in science depend the technological advances that guarantee the security of society and the machines that provide leisure to cultivate the arts. And progress in science depends in turn upon the arts and other humane studies, for they provide the aesthetic qualities that make life beautiful and help people understand history and civilization. Scientists alone cannot build a peace; we need also the knowledge, insights, and abilities of philosophers, historians, social scientists, and students of languages and literatures.[19] It is the special mission of the liberal arts college to help develop all these insights and abilities, and in a college performing this mission, those who would educate for world affairs can confidently take their places.

[19] *Ibid.,* and Harold Taylor, "Report of the President to the Board of Trustees" (Mimeographed; Bronxville, N. Y.: Sarah Lawrence College, 1957), pp. 2–3.

# Selected Bibliography

ALLERSON, HAZEL STEWART. "The Significance of World Literature Today," *College English,* VII (March 1946), 323–26.

ALMOND, GABRIEL A. *The American People and Foreign Policy.* New York: Harcourt, Brace & Co., 1950.

ALMOND, GABRIEL A., *et al. The Appeals of Communism.* Princeton, N.J.: Princeton University Press, 1954.

AMERICAN ECONOMIC ASSOCIATION, COMMITTEE ON THE UNDERGRADUATE TEACHING OF ECONOMICS AND THE TRAINING OF ECONOMISTS. HORACE TAYLOR (ed.). *The Teaching of Undergraduate Economics.* The Association, 1950.

AMERICAN POLITICAL SCIENCE ASSOCIATION. *Goals for Political Science, 1951: Report of the Committee for the Advancement of Teaching.* New York: Dryden Press, 1951.

*American Students Abroad: Goodwill Ambassadors.* Syracuse, N.Y.: Maxwell Graduate School of Citizenship and Public Affairs, Syracuse University, 1958.

ANDERSON, GEORGE L. "Cathay and the Way Thither: Oriental Literature in the World Literature Program," *Modern Language Journal,* XL (October 1956), 316–18.

ANGELL, ROBERT C. "Sociology and the World Crisis," *American Sociological Review,* XVI (December 1951), 749–57.

ASHBY, SIR ERIC. *Technology and the Academies.* London: Macmillan Co., 1958.

ASIA SOCIETY. "Asian Studies in Undergraduate Education." Mimeographed. New York: The Society, 1957.

ASSOCIATION FOR HIGHER EDUCATION. *Current Issues in Higher Education.* Proceedings of the Annual Conference on Higher Education. Washington: The Association, published annually.

ATWATER, ELTON, *et al. World Affairs: Problems and Prospects.* New York: Appleton-Century-Crofts, 1958.

AYDELOTTE, WILLIAM O. "History in a Liberal Education," *Journal of General Education,* III (October 1948), 41–48.

BAILEY, S. H. *International Studies in Modern Education.* London: Oxford University Press, 1938.

BAKER, VINCENT. "The Introductory Course in International Relations: Trends and Problems," *Universities and World Affairs,* Document No. 62. Mimeographed. New York: Carnegie Endowment for International Peace, 1954.

179

BECK, ROBERT N. "Let Us Liberalize Liberal Education," *School and Society*, LXXVII (January 3, 1953), 3–4.

BEHRENS, C. B. A. "History and the Universities," *Twentieth Century*, CLX (October 1956), 330–38.

BERKNER, LLOYD V. "Science and National Strength," *Bulletin of the Atomic Scientists*, IX (1953), 154–55 ff.

BESTOR, ARTHUR. *The Restoration of Learning*. New York: Alfred A. Knopf, 1955.

BOARDMAN, EUGENE P. *Asian Studies in Liberal Education*. Washington: Association of American Colleges, 1959.

BOWEN, HOWARD R. "Graduate Education in Economics," *American Economic Review*, XLIII (September 1953), Supplement, Part 2, 102.

BROOKINGS INSTITUTION, INTERNATIONAL STUDIES STAFF. *Report on a Conference on the Teaching of International Relations, Held at Charlottesville, Virginia, January 26–28, 1950*. [Washington]: The Institution, 1950.

BROWN, DEMING. "A Report on the Undergraduate Russian Area Programs of Nine American Universities." Mimeographed.

BULLINGTON, ROBERT A. "Summary of a Study of College Science Courses Designed for General Education," Association of American Colleges, *Bulletin*, XXXVI (May 1950), 267–72.

CAMERON, WILLIAM BRUCE; LASLEY, PHILIP; and DEWEY, RICHARD. "Who Teaches Social Psychology?" *American Sociological Review*, XV (August 1950), 553–55.

CANTRIL, HADLEY. *How Nations See Each Other: A Study in Public Opinion*. Urbana: University of Illinois Press, 1953.

CARLETON, WILLIAM G. "Wanted: Wiser Teachers of International Relations," *Journal of Higher Education*, XXV (1954), 4–5.

CARNEGIE ENDOWMENT FOR INTERNATIONAL PEACE. *Universities and World Affairs*. Mimeographed documents. New York: The Endowment, 1953–55.

CARR, E. H. *The Twenty Years' Crisis, 1919–1939*. New York: Macmillan Co., 1939.

CARR, P. O. "Approaches to the Study of World Affairs," Middle States Council for the Social Studies, *Proceedings*, 1954, pp. 15–17.

CARSON, GEORGE BARR, JR. "The Vanishing Historian," *AAUP Bulletin*, XXXIX (Autumn 1953), 474–83.

CATLIN, GEORGE. *On Political Goals*. New York: St. Martin's Press, 1957.

CHALLENER, RICHARD D., and LEE, MAURICE, JR. "History and the Social Sciences: The Problem of Communications; Notes on a Conference Held by the Social Science Research Council," *American Historical Review*, LXII (January 1956), 331–38.

CHALMERS, GORDON KEITH. "The Break in Liberalism," Association of American Colleges, *Bulletin*, XXXII (October 1946), 378–86.

CHEVALLIER, J.-J. "L'enseignement des relations internationales," *L'enseignement des Sciences Sociales en France.* [Paris]: Unesco, 1953.

CLEVELAND, HARLAN. "The Real International World and the Academic Lag," ROY A. PRICE (ed.), *New Viewpoints in the Social Sciences,* pp. 172–88. Twenty-eighth Yearbook of the National Council for the Social Studies. Washington: The Council, 1958.

COHEN, I. BERNARD, and WATSON, FLETCHER G. (eds.). *General Education in Science.* Cambridge, Mass.: Harvard University Press, 1952.

COLE, CHARLES C., JR. "History in a General Education Program at Columbia College," *Journal of Higher Education,* XXVII (October 1956), 359–63.

COLE, FRED. *International Relations in Institutions of Higher Education in the South.* Washington: American Council on Education, 1958.

CONANT, JAMES B. *The American High School Today.* New York: McGraw-Hill Book Co., 1959.

"Conference on the Teaching of International Law," *American Journal of International Law,* LI (January 1957), 92–94.

CORBETT, PERCY E. *The Study of International Law.* New York: Doubleday & Co., 1955.

DAGHLIAN, PHILIP B., and FRENZ, HORST. "Evolution of World Literature Course," *College English,* XII (December 1950), 150–53.

DAY, EDMUND E. "Notes on the Reorientation of Liberal Education," Association of American Colleges, *Bulletin,* XXXII (October 1946), 338–45.

DEAN, VERA MICHELES. *The American Student and the Non-Western World.* Cambridge, Mass.: Harvard University Press, 1956.

DEUTSCH, KARL W., et al. *Political Community and the North Atlantic Area.* Princeton, N.J.: Princeton University Press, 1957.

"Developing Cultural Understanding Through Foreign Language Study: A Report of the MLA Interdisciplinary Seminar in Language and Culture," *PMLA,* LXVIII (December 1953), 1196–1218.

DE VISSCHER, CHARLES. *Theory and Reality in Public International Law.* Translated by PERCY E. CORBETT. Princeton, N.J.: Princeton University Press, 1957.

DE VISSCHER, PAUL. "Conference on the Teaching of International Law," *The Yearbook of World Affairs, 1957,* pp. 257–72. London: Stevens & Sons, 1957.

DODDS, HAROLD W. "Liberal Arts, Challenge to Communism," Association of American Colleges, *Bulletin,* XXXV (October 1949), 336–45.

DOYLE, HENRY GRATTAN. "Will Translation Suffice?" Language Leaflet No. 10. Washington: George Washington University, 1940.

DUNN, FREDERICK S. "The Scope of International Relations," *World Politics,* I (October 1948), 142–46.

———. *War and the Minds of Men.* New York: Harper & Bros., 1950.

EDUCATIONAL POLICIES COMMISSION. *The Contemporary Challenge to American Education*. Washington: The Commission, 1958.

EHRMANN, HENRY W. (ed.). *The Teaching of the Social Sciences in the United States*. Paris: Unesco, 1954.

EISENHOWER, MILTON S. "Education for International Understanding," *Educational Record*, XXXV (October 1954), 243–49.

FALK, SIGNI. "International Understanding: An Experiment in Freshman English," *College English*, VIII (January 1947), 196–203.

FERRISS, ABBOTT L. "'Introductory Sociology' in the South-eastern States: 1950," *Social Forces*, XXIX (March 1951), 295–301.

*Final Report of the Southeastern Assembly on the United States and the Far East*. Atlanta, Ga.: Emory University, 1958.

FINNEY, NAT S. "The Threat to Atomic Science," *Bulletin of the Atomic Scientists*, X (1954), 285–86 ff.

FOSDICK, DOROTHY. "Higher Education and World Affairs," *Current Issues in Higher Education*, pp. 18–25. Washington: Association for Higher Education, 1955.

FULLER, C. DALE. *Training of Specialists in International Relations*. Washington: American Council on Education, 1957.

*General Education in a Free Society: Report of the Harvard Committee*. Cambridge, Mass.: Harvard University Press, 1945.

GOODWIN, GEOFFREY L. *The University Teaching of International Relations*. Oxford: Blackwell, 1951.

GOULD, SAMUEL B. "Education's Mount Everest," *Antioch Notes*, XXXII (May 15, 1955), 3–4.

———. "The University's Stake in Educational Travel," *The American Student Abroad 1956–57*, pp. 5–7. New York: Council on Student Travel [1958].

"Great Issues Course at Dartmouth College," *American Political Science Review*, XLIII (February 1949), 91–94.

GROBSTEIN, CLIFFORD. "Federal Research and Development: Prospects 1954," *Bulletin of the Atomic Scientists*, IX (1953), 299–304.

GYORGY, ANDRE, and GIBBS, HUBERT L. *Problems in International Relations*. New York: Prentice-Hall, 1955.

HAAS, ERNEST B., and WHITING, ALLEN S. *Dynamics of International Relations*. New York: McGraw-Hill Book Co., 1956.

HADDOW, ANNA. *Political Science in American Colleges and Universities, 1636–1900*. New York: Appleton-Century Co., 1939.

HALLE, LOUIS J. "History and the Present," *Virginia Quarterly Review*, XXXI (Fall 1955), 497–504.

HANSON, A. H. "Politics as a University Discipline," *Universities Quarterly*, VIII (November 1953), 34–43.

HIGH, JAMES. "History in General Education," *Social Education*, XXI (February 1957), 56–58.

HOULE, CYRIL O., and NELSON, CHARLES A. *The University, the Citizen, and World Affairs.* Washington: American Council on Education, 1956.

INKELES, ALEX. "Understanding a Foreign Society: A Sociologist's View," *World Politics,* III (January 1951), 269–80.

INSTITUTE OF INTERNATIONAL EDUCATION. *News Bulletin* (New York), published monthly September through May.

JESSUP, PHILIP. "Report of the Committee on Review of the Charter of the United Nations," *Proceedings and Committee Reports of the American Branch of the International Law Association, 1955–1956,* pp. 69–81. New York: New York University Law Center, 1956.

———. *Transnational Law.* New Haven, Conn.: Yale University Press, 1956.

JOHNSTON, MARJORIE C. "How Can Modern Language Teaching Promote International Understanding?" National Association of Secondary-School Principals, *Bulletin,* XL (December 1956), 70–85.

JONES, HOWARD MUMFORD. "Education and One World," LYMAN BRYSON, LOUIS FINKELSTEIN, and R. M. MacIVER (eds.), *Goals for American Education: Ninth Symposium,* pp. 213–33. ("Conference on Science, Philosophy and Religion Series.") New York: Harper & Bros., 1950.

KENNAN, GEORGE F. *American Diplomacy 1900–1950.* Chicago: University of Chicago Press, 1951.

KIRK, GRAYSON L. *The Study of International Relations in American Colleges and Universities.* New York: Council on Foreign Relations, 1947.

———. "The Study of International Relations in American Universities," *Southern University Conference Proceedings 1947,* pp 49–58. New Orleans, La.: The Conference, 1947.

KLINE, MORRIS. "Freshman Mathematics as an Integral Part of Western Culture," *American Mathematical Monthly,* LXI (May 1954), 295–306.

———. *Mathematics in Western Culture.* New York: Oxford University Press, 1953.

KLINEBERG, OTTO. *Tensions Affecting International Understanding.* New York: Social Science Research Council, 1950.

KNORR, KLAUS. "Economics and International Relations: A Problem in Teaching," *Political Science Quarterly,* LXII (December 1947), 552–68.

LASSWELL, HAROLD. *World Politics and Personal Insecurity.* New York: McGraw-Hill Book Co., 1935.

LAWSON, S. "Colgate Plan for Improving Student Writing," Association of American Colleges, *Bulletin,* XXXIX (May 1953), 288–90.

LEFEVER, ERNEST. *Ethics and United States Foreign Policy.* New York: Meridian Books, 1957.

LIPPMANN, WALTER. "The Changing Times," LEONARD D. WHITE (ed.), *The State of the Social Sciences,* pp. 340–47. Chicago: University of Chicago Press, 1956.

———. *The Public Philosophy.* Boston: Little, Brown & Co., 1956.

MANNING, C. A. W. *The University Teaching of Social Sciences: International Relations.* Paris: Unesco, 1954.

MARTIN, CHARLES E. "The Teaching of International Law from the Viewpoint of Political Science Programs, Graduate and Undergraduate," University of Washington Institute of International Affairs, Bulletin No. 12, July 1954. Mimeographed.

McCONNELL, T. R. "General Education: An Analysis," NELSON B. HENRY (ed.), *The Fifty-first Yearbook of the National Society for the Study of Education, Part I: General Education,* pp. 1–19. Chicago: University of Chicago Press, 1952.

McGRATH, EARL J. (ed.). *The Humanities in General Education.* Dubuque, Iowa: William C. Brown Co., 1949.

———. *Science in General Education.* Dubuque, Iowa: William C. Brown Co., 1948.

———. *Social Science in General Education.* Dubuque, Iowa: William C. Brown Co., 1948.

McGRATH, EARL J., and RUSSELL, CHARLES H. *Are Liberal Arts Colleges Becoming Professional Schools?* New York: Teachers College, Columbia University, 1958.

MILDENBERGER, KENNETH W. *Status of Foreign Language Study in American Elementary Schools in 1955.* Washington: U.S. Office of Education, Department of Health, Education, and Welfare, 1955.

MODERN LANGUAGE ASSOCIATION. *The FL Program.* Mimeographed. New York: The Association, 1954———.

MORGENTHAU, HANS J. "Area Studies and the Study of International Relations," *International Social Science Bulletin,* IV (1952), 3–11.

———. *In Defense of the National Interest.* New York: Alfred A. Knopf, 1951.

MORGENTHAU, HANS J., and THOMPSON, KENNETH W. *Principles and Problems of International Politics.* New York: Alfred A. Knopf, 1950.

MOSSE, GEORGE L. "Freshman History: Reality or Metaphysics?" *The Social Studies,* XLIX (March 1949), 99–103.

MUMFORD, LEWIS. "The Transformations of Man," ANDREW A. FREEMAN (ed.), *Brainpower Quest,* pp. 75–88. New York: Macmillan Co., 1957.

"National Programs of International Cultural Relations," *International Conciliation,* No. 642 (June 1950), pp. 301–36.

NEWMAN, JOHN HENRY CARDINAL. *The Idea of a University* (1852), Discourse VII.

NICOLSON, HAROLD. *Diplomacy.* London: Oxford University Press, 1950.

NORTHROP, F. S. C. "Education for Intercultural Understanding," *Journal of Higher Education,* XVIII (April 1947), 177–81

NOSTRAND, HOWARD LEE. "On Teaching a Foreign Culture," *Modern Language Journal,* XL (October 1956), 297–301.

NOSTRAND, HOWARD LEE, and BROWN, FRANCIS J. (eds.). *The Role of Colleges and Universities in International Understanding.* Washington: American Council on Education, 1949.

NOWELL, CHARLES E. "Has the Past a Place in History?" *Journal of Modern History,* XXIV (December 1952), 331–40.

ODEGAARD, CHARLES E. "MLA Interdisciplinary Seminar on Language and Culture," *Modern Language Journal,* XXXVIII (April 1954), 165–69.

OGBURN, WILLIAM FIELDING (ed.). *Technology and International Relations.* Chicago: University of Chicago Press, 1949.

PALMER, NORMAN D., and PERKINS, HOWARD C. *International Relations.* 2d ed. Boston: Houghton Mifflin Co., 1957.

PALMER, THOMAS W., JR. "An Area Approach for the Language Professor," *Modern Language Journal,* XL (January 1956), 31–33.

PANOFSKY, ERWIN. "In Defense of the Ivory Tower," *Harvard Alumni Bulletin,* LIX (July 6, 1957), 706–10.

PARKER, WILLIAM R. "Why a Foreign Language Requirement?" *College and University,* XXXIII (Winter 1957), 189–203.

PEYRE, HENRI. "The Need for Language Study in America Today," *Modern Language Journal,* XL (October 1956), 323–34.

PFEFFER, J. ALLEN. "Modern Languages in the American College Curriculum," *Modern Language Journal,* XXXIX (February 1955), 64–68.

PRICE, DONALD K. *Government in Science.* New York: New York University Press, 1954.

*Proceedings of the American Society of International Law.* Washington: The Society, published annually.

RANDALL, J. G. "Historianship," *American Historical Review,* LVIII (May 1953), 249–64.

RASHDALL, HASTINGS. *The Universities of Europe in the Middle Ages.* Oxford: Clarendon Press, 1936.

ROBSON, WILLIAM A. *The University Teaching of Social Sciences: Political Science.* [Paris]: Unesco, 1954.

SCHILLING, HAROLD K. "What Should Be the Balance between Liberal and Specialized Education?" *Current Issues in Higher Education,* pp. 78–82. Washington: Association for Higher Education, 1955.

SCHLEICHER, CHARLES. *Introduction to International Relations.* New York: Prentice-Hall, 1954.

SCHUMAN, FREDERICK L. *International Politics.* New York: McGraw-Hill Book Co., 1933; 6th ed., 1958.

SCHWARZENBERGER, GEORG. *Power Politics.* New York: Frederick Praeger, 1951.

SHAYON, ROBERT LEWIS. "Report from the Grass-Roots," *Saturday Review,* XLI (September 13, 1958), 15–17 ff.

SHILS, EDWARD A. "Scientists, Administrators, and Politicians: The Report of the Riehlman Committee," *Bulletin of the Atomic Scientists,* X (1954), 371–74.

SINGER, MILTON (ed.). *Introducing India in Liberal Education.* Chicago: University of Chicago Press, 1957.

SMUCKLER, RALPH H. "The Region of Isolationism," *American Political Science Review,* XLVII (December 1953), 386–401.

SNYDER, HAROLD E. "What Are Some of the More Effective Ways of Reshaping Programs of General Education To Equip Students More Adequately To Cope with America's Changing Role in International Affairs?" *Current Issues in Higher Education,* pp. 312–13. Washington: Association for Higher Education, 1955.

SNYDER, RICHARD C.; BRUCK, H. W.; and SAPIN, BURTON. *Decision-Making as an Approach to the Study of International Politics.* ("Foreign Policy Analysis Series," No. 3.) Princeton, N.J.: Organizational Behavior Section, Princeton University, 1954.

SOMERVELL, D. C. "History as a University Subject," *Universities Quarterly,* VII (February 1953), 147–50.

STAKMAN, E. C. "Science and International Understanding," *School Science and Mathematics,* LII (June 1952), 11–18.

STEARNS, RAYMOND P. "College History and Its New Approaches," *School and Society,* LXXXII (August 20, 1955), 49–55.

SYMONS, FARRELL. *Courses on International Affairs in American Colleges, 1930–31.* Boston: World Peace Foundation, 1931.

TAYLOR, HAROLD. "The Aims of Education," *College English,* XVIII (February 1957), 245–51.

TAYLOR, HORACE. "The Teaching of Economics in the United States," *The University Teaching of Social Sciences: Economics.* [Paris]: Unesco, 1954.

*The Teaching of the Social Sciences in the United States.* Paris: Unesco, 1954.

TEAD, ORDWAY. "Effective Learning in College," *Journal of Chemical Education,* XXIX (November 1952), 565–70.

TOYNBEE, ARNOLD. "The Writing of History," *Times Literary Supplement* (London), August 15, 1958, p. xxv.

TREVOR-ROPER, H. R. "Arnold Toynbee's Millennium," *Encounter,* VIII (June 1957), 14–27.

TYRRELL, WILLIAM G. "Developing International Understanding in the First Two Years of College," HOWARD R. ANDERSON (ed.), *Approaches to an Understanding of World Affairs,* Twenty-fifth Yearbook of the National Council for the Social Studies, pp. 385–95. Washington: The Council, 1954.

U.S. OFFICE OF EDUCATION. *Modern Foreign Languages in the High School.* Washington: Government Printing Office, 1958.

VAN DOREN, MARK. *Liberal Education.* New York: Henry Holt & Co., 1943.

VAN DYKE, VERNON. *International Politics.* New York: Appleton-Century-Crofts, 1957.

——— (ed.). *Some Approaches and Concepts Used in the Teaching of International Politics.* Iowa City: State University of Iowa Press, 1957.

VLEKKE, B. H. M. *On the Study of International Political Science.* London: David Davies Memorial Institute of International Studies [1957].

WALDO, DWIGHT. *Political Science in the United States of America.* Paris: Unesco, 1956.

WARE, EDITH E. *The Study of International Relations in the United States, Survey for 1934.* New York: Columbia University Press, 1934.

WASHTON, NATHAN S. "A Survey of Science Courses for General Education in Colleges," American Association of Colleges, *Bulletin,* XXXIV (October 1948), 285–94.

WEAVER, EDWARD K., *et al.* "Review of Recent Research in the Teaching of Science at the College," *Science Education,* XL (December 1956), 350–57.

WHITE, LEONARD D. (ed.). *The State of the Social Sciences.* Chicago: University of Chicago Press, 1956.

WILCOX, FRANCIS O. "Education for Overseasmanship," *NEA Journal,* XLVI (November 1957), 505.

———. "Foreign Policy and Some Implications for Education," U.S. Department of State, *Bulletin,* XXXVII (July 29, 1957), 179–85.

WILSON, ARTHUR M. "Dartmouth's Venture in Great Issues," *Higher Education,* IV (May 15, 1948), 209–10.

WILSON, HOWARD E. *American College Life as Education in World Outlook.* Washington: American Council on Education, 1956.

———. *Universities and World Affairs.* New York: Carnegie Endowment for International Peace, 1951.

WOODWARD, E. L. *The Study of International Relations at a University.* Oxford: Clarendon Press, 1948.

WRIGHT, QUINCY. *Contemporary International Law: A Balance Sheet.* New York: Doubleday & Co., 1955.

———. *The Study of International Relations.* New York: Appleton-Century-Crofts, 1955.

———. *A Study of War.* 2 vols. Chicago: University of Chicago Press, 1942.

———. "The Teaching of International Law in the Postwar World," *Proceedings of the Eighth Conference on the Teaching of International Law and Related Subjects,* pp. 22–28. Washington: Carnegie Endowment for International Peace, 1946.

WRISTON, HENRY M. "Education and the National Interest," *Foreign Affairs,* XXXV (July 1957), 564–80.

YOUNG, ROLAND (ed.). *Approaches to the Study of Politics.* Evanston, Ill.: Northwestern University Press, 1958.

ZIMMERN, SIR ALFRED. "Education and International Goodwill," *The Sixth Earl Grey Memorial Lecture.* London: Oxford University Press, 1924.

———. "International Understanding and the American College," Sweet Briar College, *The Role of the Colleges in Promoting Peace through International Understanding.* Sweet Briar, Va.: The College, 1948.

———. "Introductory Report to the Discussions in 1935," *University Teaching of International Relations.* Paris: International Institute of Intellectual Cooperation, 1939.

# Index

specialists and nonspecialists and that all students should learn something about the subject to be truly educated in this century. He gives many examples of ways in which a great variety of programs and courses can contribute to students' knowledge and understanding of world affairs.

Faculty members and administrators will find helpful the suggestions and concrete examples

- for broadening and improving course content,
- for establishing a course in world affairs,
- for programs for major study.

*Dr. Swift, who has been a visiting lecturer at both Harvard and Yale Universities, is Associate Professor of Government at New York University, teaching in the Washington Square College of Arts and Science and the Graduate School of Arts and Science.*

THE CARNEGIE ENDOWMENT FOR INTERNATIONAL PEACE launched in 1950 a program of study of American universities and world affairs. As a part of this program 60 institutions completed self-surveys, in which they made an exploratory inventory and an analysis of their resources and activities bearing on world affairs. To obtain an interpretation of the survey experience on these widely varied campuses, the Endowment requested a number of specialists to prepare volumes on topics which had been revealed as particularly important. The resulting series of books, of which this is one, are listed on the back of this jacket.

Date Due